MW01617987

Praise for *Badge Unbroken*

"Robert Hall has never been given the opportunity to tell his side of the story in the controversial roller coaster ride of his tenure at the Tupelo Police Department – until now. With the expert assistance of Sandy Grisham, this is a blow-by-blow account of the ups and downs and final ascent of one man's battle to end up on top."

Jack Reed, Jr.

Mayor of Tupelo 2009–2013

"Every story and reflection took me to the place and made the words transplant me into a communal experience. The power of Robert Hall's journey repeatedly validated how God is ever present in the lives of his children. God showed up and showed out over and over again. Robert enjoyed numerous advancement opportunities, and they were all positive. While he consistently reflected on what he didn't have, he, in fact, had all that he needed. This story deserves a national voice; it is a painful journey shared by many in all fields of work, hope, and life."

Dr. Tonea Stewart

Actress, author, and former dean, Alabama State University

"*Badge Unbroken* reads like an intriguing novel set in the Mississippi world of lingering racial prejudice. Holding the reader's attention from beginning to end, Hall, along with Sandy Grisham, tells a compelling story of a boy in Tupelo, Mississippi, who dreamed of being a cop, finding that dream, and then having it snatched away by fellow white police officers filled with jealousy and resentment. Hall's story of courage, honor, and eternal optimism is a must-read for anyone involved in law enforcement or dedicated to making the world around them a better place."

Mary Ann Strong Connell

Author, An Unforeseen Life

"In Mississippi's long, unsavory history of racism and civil rights abuse, Tupelo, under enlightened leadership, seemed to stand out as an island of civility and reason. *Badge Unbroken* rips the curtain off that façade of decency to lay bare the same old prejudice and discrimination in, of all places, the police department. Those sworn to uphold equal justice under the law operated with deep animosity directed towards one of their own. Robert Hall's story of courage in the face of mistreatment, false accusations, even betrayal serves as a powerful reminder that we still have a long way to go."

Dr. Lucie Bridgforth

Professor emerita, Northwest Mississippi Community College

"Robert Hall's story is—above all—a story of remarkable strength of character, perseverance and serenity. It's the story of growing up black in the South and overcoming her institutional racial barriers to become deputy police chief in Tupelo, Mississippi, one of that state's larger cities. For ulterior reasons not completely revealed to him, Robert was unfairly impeached for 'going easy' on a black member of his church who was suspected of a hit-and-run. Despite allegations of racial favoritism and even trumped-up perjury charges, Robert kept his faith in the system and the fairness of human nature. When they failed him, Robert bounced back and found purpose in other ways to help his fellow man."

Richard "Dickie" Scruggs

Founder, Second Chance Mississippi

"Deputy Chief Robert Hall was viciously attacked and betrayed with lies against his character and career, but he is no victim. *Badge Unbroken* is a personal history of resilience, grace, and strength overcoming mendacity and bigotry. This is a story of racial injustice as old as Mississippi and as fresh as the 21st Century, told in a relatable voice, as though he were sitting in your living room. I first knew Robert Hall as a young officer in Tupelo while I was one of the city's outside attorneys. Robert was a straight arrow then, and after all of his travails, he is still on target with *Badge Unbroken*."

Rear Admiral Jamie Barnett

United States Navy

"*Badge Unbroken* is a riveting book that captures the heart and soul of Robert's intriguing life. He endured, he persevered – his foundation of a strong and loving family, his faith, and his community sustained him through the difficulties he faced with his career. I am so proud of the people who have/had the infamous "Tupelo Spirit"; the people who stood up for Robert; the people who gave willingly to keep he and his family afloat; the people who used their influence. This book should be a mandatory read for law enforcement, for students, for pastors, etc., because it teaches true leadership, forgiveness, and redemption in overcoming racial discord."

Juanita Gambrell Floyd

Author and Senior Vice President, CREATE Foundation

"In a word...compelling. Robert Hall and I are about the same age. We were both born and grew up in the south. He grew up in Mississippi, and I grew up in Alabama. Our lives growing up were completely different because of *one* thing...the color of our skin. That's it! This was a compelling read that should be required reading of every white man in America. It was truly a page-turner. We like to say we have made strides in regard to racism...and maybe we have...but we have a long way to go. Robert Hall is a hero."

Dr. Chuck Strong

Former vice president, Northwest Mississippi Community College

"*Badge Unbroken* offers insights into the human condition. How can people be so cruel and hurtful to each other based on the color of their skin? How does a person survive such jealousy, racism and betrayal and remain committed to his life goals to serve others in the face of such adversity? Robert Hall and Sandy Grisham lay out Robert's life story as a man driven to serve others even though he experienced many roadblocks along the way. Despite adversities, he managed to keep his focus on making life better for all people. The authors give us many life questions to ponder. You will be inspired!"

Dr. Ron Evenson

Former mayor, Houston, Minnesota

"Robert Hall's story is a must-read for all Southerners. A story of grit and determination in the face of adversity and racial injustice. Hall dedicated his life to serve and protect a society that was often unfair and corrupt. Despite the odds and setbacks, Hall proved himself to be not only a man of integrity, but a shining example to us all."

Michelle Mason

Managing director, First Commercial Bank

"The two things that are most apparent in Robert Hall's life are his courage and his willingness not to return evil for evil. His resilience and faith are as unwavering as this book is compelling."

Reverend Christopher Powell

Retired Episcopal priest

BADGE UNBROKEN

THE ROBERT HALL STORY

SANDY GRISHAM and ROBERT HALL

Badge Unbroken: The Robert Hall Story © copyright, 2025, by Sandy Grisham and Robert Hall. No part of this book may be reproduced without the express, written consent of the publisher except in the case of brief quotations embodied in critical articles and reviews.

Some names have been changed to protect the privacy of those involved.

For more information, contact Nautilus Publishing, 155 CR 418, Oxford, MS, 38655

ISBN: 978-1-949455-62-5

First Edition

Library of Congress Cataloging-in-Publication Data has been applied for.
Printed in the United States of America

10 9 8 7 6 5 4 3 2 1

Interior design: Sinclair Guenther
Cover design: Carroll Chiles-Moore

We'd like to dedicate this book to our parents.

To B.T. and Florine Hall, and especially to Robert's mom, who kept saying, "You aren't supposed to be here."

And to Sandy's parents, Ruth and Wally Hopper, who said, "We are late bloomers." But I'm 86 years old. Really, Daddy?

Table of Contents

A Note from Robert

To our readers:

Life isn't always fair. This story is for those of you who have been unfairly treated, or who can expect to be unfairly treated because of the color of your skin or your sex or your religion or any of the other myriad number of ways in which the human race divides itself.

This book is also written for the reader interested in law enforcement, the legal field, for students and professors of criminal justice, but most of all, for the citizens in very real communities where some people can be mistreated because of their skin color.

It is a real story of unfair treatment, discrimination, and survival.

Introduction

It was an ordinary early October evening as I drove my pickup truck down the road toward Tupelo. Although I was going from my safe home in a rural area of Mississippi to the BanCorp South Arena in the heart of my hometown, nothing was emotionally "safe" about this evening.

I pulled into the parking lot of the large facility where performers like Elton John sang and played their hearts out to eager audiences. There were cars of every age, size, and color in that huge parking lot, and I felt more and more tension the closer I got to the building. My heart pounded, my breathing was short, and I felt almost nauseated.

This meeting had been called to pursue the city's issues with me.

I entered the large meeting room where about 60 percent of the audience was African-American and the rest were white. All 200 seats in the room were taken with folks who were shaking hands and chatting quietly. People from all over the county lined the walls, standing somewhat relaxed, but glancing around to see who was there. As I entered, a hush fell over the crowd. You could tell they knew who I was – whether I had met them or not.

I am Robert Earl Hall, the policeman fired from the Tupelo Police Department and charged with "protecting" a member of my own race at the expense of the city's safety.

It was the second week of October, and Allan Denton's case was splashed all over the pages of the local newspaper. I had been portrayed as the bad black cop who had not arrested a drunk black guy who had hit a teenager on a bike and run away from the scene.

The TPD suspended me and put me in offices far away from the police station. And they did not pay me.

I kept thinking this nightmare would end, and things would go back to normal soon. Justice would prevail.

I was wrong.

The city council was mired in these racial issues with the NAACP. The board decided to have a meeting to clear the air and get the citizens' opinions of this situation. That's the way Tupelo does things – they get the issues out in the public and try to work toward common ground. They'd been doing this for decades, and that's the way they would do it in my case. I had hopes for that anyway.

The meeting was set for Thursday, October 12, 2006.

Speakers included the head of the NAACP, some council members, and others. The "other" that most interested me was my partner and best friend, a white officer named Cliff Hardy.

An article in the *Northeast Mississippi Daily Journal* said it all: "Fellow Officer Supports Hall".

Cliff was recognized to speak by the head of the council. These are his exact words. I am including it all, not only because it is relevant, but because it is also eloquent. And publicly, I repeat what I have said to him many times since: "Thank you, Cliff."

The leader introduced him. "Cliff Hardy, Detective, Tupelo Police Department." After a brief buzz in the audience, the room was silent. Cliff pulled himself up to his full height and began to read his statement.

"I have served as a sworn officer for the Tupelo Police Department for over nineteen years. Over the years I have had occasion many times to address issues affecting the department with aldermen, councilmen, mayors, and other elected officials. I can honestly say that, out of loyalty to the TPD, I never took advantage of the opportunities that arose. However, as I near the end of my career I find myself in a position where I cannot in good conscience remain silent. I realize that there are many sensitive issues here that demand attention and many dynamics at work. I could remain silent, as I have in the past, and let these issues be worked out by others. But I know that if I did, I could not look my children in the eyes, and even more so, I fear [the] words that would be spoken by my Savior when I one day stand before Him and give account.

"The specific issue I will address is the persecution of Robert Hall. I realize that 'persecute' is a very strong word, but I do not hesitate to use it based on its definition as listed in the American Heritage Dictionary: 'To oppress or harass with ill-treatment, especially because of race, religion, gender, sexual orientation, or beliefs.' I have no doubt that there are many who say that I am biased due to my close friendship with Robert. I have spent the majority of the past nineteen years watching his back, as he watched mine in dangerous situations. However, our friendship does not change the facts of his predicament one bit.

"Robert also has over nineteen years of service with the TPD. In those years, he has not once received formal discipline for the way he performed his duty. I cannot begin to list the number of murderers, bank robbers, rapists, and other serious felons that he has been responsible for getting off the streets of Tupelo. It was through his ability, hard work, dedication to duty, and the personal sacrifice of time that should have been spent with his family that Robert progressed to the top of his profession with the TPD. I believe it was in 2002 that Robert was summoned to then-Mayor Larry Otis's office, where he was appointed to deputy chief of the TPD, at the same time that Chief received his appointment.

"To say that the time since has been turbulent would be an understatement. Robert's tenure as deputy chief has been marked with contention. His efforts to install fair and impartial continuity within the Tupelo Police Department has been challenged at every turn and given rise to powerful critics who resist any form of change from the 'old way of doing things.' Such areas include hiring, promotions, lateral transfers, the handling of citizen complaints, Officers Early Warning System, Community-Oriented Policing, and many more.

"The result of his determined effort to improve the quality of service delivered by the Tupelo PD has led us to this moment in time. This good man now stands with his reputation in question, his pay cut, and his future uncertain. He has had to stand silently by as the system that he has served so faithfully grinds inexorably forward towards his ruin, reminiscent of times past when anyone of color challenged authority and 'went too far'.

"I am aware that this is a bold statement to make, and I do not take it lightly. We can only imagine what he has been subjected to in these past few months. I personally experienced a taste of what he has been through. I was approached very recently by two investigators with the MBI and asked to give a statement concerning an incident I witnessed involving Robert.

"I met these two at the Lee County Justice Center while I was on duty. After entering the room where the interview was to take place, I was immediately asked if I was armed. It was obvious that I was, in that I did not have a jacket on and my weapon and badge were in plain sight, and I had already confirmed both my name, rank, and standing with the TPD. I was asked to relinquish my weapon for the interview and place it in an unsecured bathroom. I respectfully declined to do so and gave an explanation why.

"One of the investigators then began asking me inane questions regarding my life and career. After I asked for the interview to begin, the same investigator became very belligerent and attempted to intimidate me with statements of how poor my attitude was towards him. The second investigator then advised me of my rights under Miranda. I asked him if I was under investigation, and his answer was vague – something to the effect that anything could happen. When he completed the advisement, I then requested my lawyer to be present. They both questioned me as to why, stating that they just needed a statement from me. I replied that if they felt it was necessary to advise me of my constitutional rights, I felt it necessary to take advantage of what they afforded. One of the investigators then took the rights waiver and tore it up, saying something to the effect of, 'Now we can proceed.' Seeing that they appeared to have little regard for the rights of others, I ended the meeting and left their presence.

"I was later confronted by my supervisor, who asked if they, the MBI, [had escorted] me from the building that day, which of course they did not. When I later asked about who made the false statement, I was informed that the two MBI investigators had claimed it and that was verified by [the] Sheriff. Again, being on the receiving end of such treatment, I can only imagine what Robert has been through.

"Even so, I have not lost hope in his cause. I know that there is fast approaching a day when he and his advocates will have an opportunity to bring all things to light. However, I am very anxious as to what damages will result before the truth in all this is allowed to come forth. Therefore I implore you to give this situation the highest priority. I encourage you to be thorough and relentless in searching for the truth. This, I assure you, is what Robert Hall desires and what he has earned.

"It was Plato who said, 'We can easily forgive a child who is afraid of the dark; the real tragedy of life is when men are afraid of the light.'"

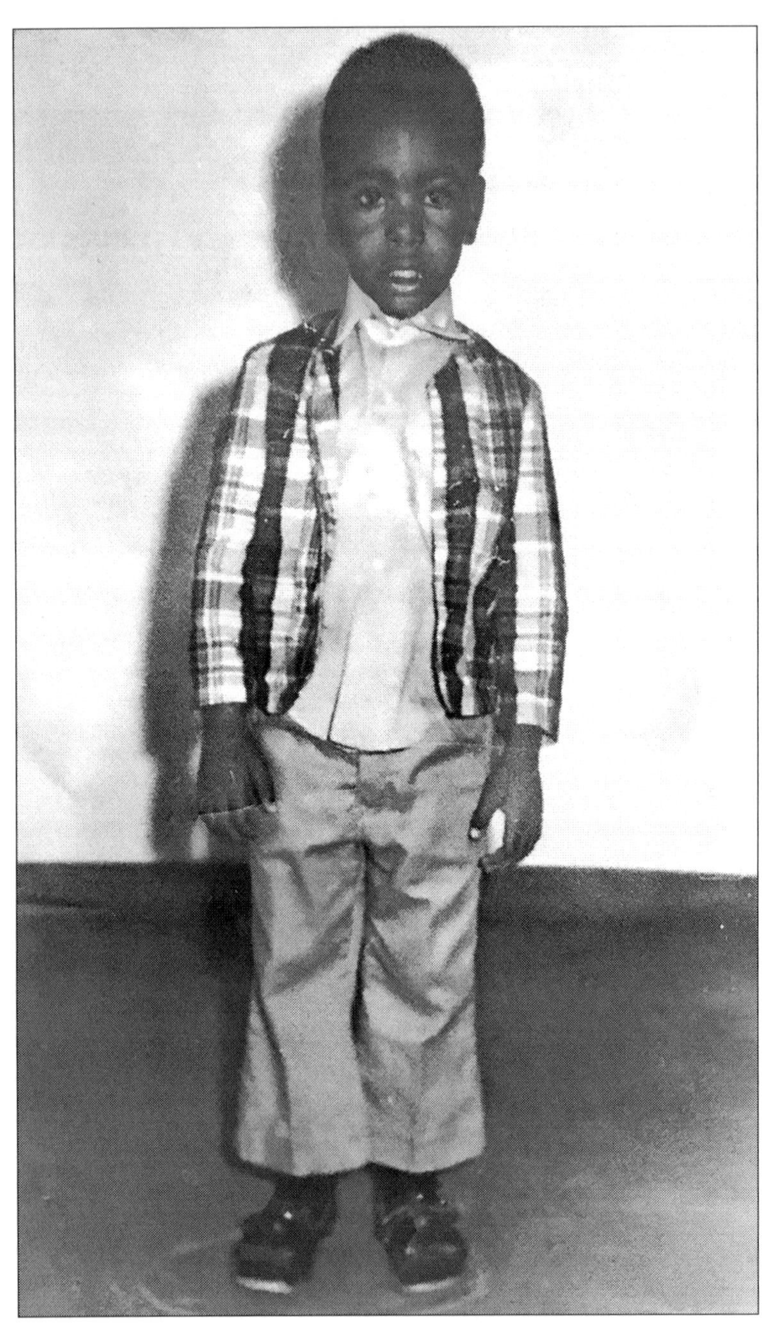

Robert on the first day of kindergarten

Chapter One

I'm Not Supposed to Be Here

I am Robert Earl Hall, born on September 26, 1966, in Tupelo, Mississippi. I am a black man, raised in a black family with lots and lots of cousins. We weren't rich; we weren't even middle class. We're folks who did the hard scrabble work like digging in sweating-hot weather in the summer or raining, freezing, cold winters for mostly less than minimum wage. Or maybe we wrung the necks of chickens daily so they could be cut up and sold to folks. We went to church, and we went to work, and we took care of each other. We knew God cared about us, and we tried to follow his words.

Sometimes we didn't do such a good job, but we still tried.

My daddy was born in 1913 and he was ten years older than my momma. But Daddy took care of her like she was a queen. And she cared for him, too, and the six kids and her uncle who lived in our small clapboard house in Saltillo, Mississippi.

It was just 1966, and I wasn't around yet, but I can just hear my momma saying, "Lordy, Lordy – I *can't* be pregnant. I got these five kids.... Bennie's already 12! And Diane is just 5! I just *can't* be pregnant again! I been taking those new pills – birth control pills! Lordy, Lordy!"

Well, she was, and I'm the product of those pills that didn't work. She always used to tell me, "You aren't supposed to be here, Robert. You're not supposed to be here."

Surprising thing, though. My mom wasn't supposed to live past 10 or 12 years old. She told me not long before she died that her days were numbered when she was a kid, but she didn't tell me what would cause her to die this early. She did have a very long life – she celebrated ninety-four birthdays before she went to her heavenly father. When I asked my sister Berta Mae if she knew that Mom was supposed to die early, she said she did, but had no idea what the cause was either.

If you don't ask those questions when they're living, you can't get the answers when they're gone, can you?

I guess we were both "not supposed to be", but we sure were anyway.

I am the youngest of that Hall family. And I guess I was kind of spoiled. I don't know. All I know is that we were surrounded by love and caring folks. I always said I lived in a "neighborhood of parents" because all the adults took care of all the kids. I couldn't misbehave at all anywhere before someone else's folks would see me and yell out, "Robert, you just stop that right now!" And when I skedaddled home, my mom or dad already knew what I had done.

It was a very comfortable place to grow up.... We all were alike and all related and all helped each other whenever we could.

My earliest memories are of a childhood in a farm community. Daddy worked as a sharecropper, and Momma cleaned the homes of white families. Together they worked and put up a garden, and, in the fall, Momma would sweat bullets in the hot kitchen all day. First, she'd wash, then slice those tomatoes, then cut them into whatever sized chunks she wanted. I can remember the steam coming out of that pot that cleaned those jars and got them ready for what we had harvested. It was like being in a sauna – steamy and hot through and through. Once Momma skinned and cut those red tomatoes, she added a little salt and some other stuff maybe, and then those slippery, thin lids went on top, and the ring got screwed around the top of the jar. At last, she would put all the jars into the canner on the stove and cook them until the lid snapped tight on the jar.

Our shelves were beautiful all winter with those red jars of tomatoes. Green beans sat next to them, and a raft of other veggies were there, too.

That's what I remember. And believe me, in the dark cold days of winter, those beans and tomatoes were like manna from heaven.

Besides being a great father, my dad was a deacon of the church and a very well-respected man in the community. He did not drink, and he was a hard-working man – a man who took good care of his wife and family. And he took care of the neighborhood, too.

Every year, Daddy would have a hog killing at our place, and all the folks from around us would come and help and then share in the kill.

Dad raised big pigs. I mean, to a kid, those were some big pigs. Every year he would slaughter a whole pig for the entire community to share. I remember it well.

I guess if you aren't born or raised in the country, seeing a pig get slaughtered isn't very pretty, but when you are hungry in the winter, that slaughtered meat is a beautiful sight.

Bennie was the best shot in the area, drunk or sober, so it was his job to shoot the best pig Dad could choose from the lot. When he came in late from a night of carousing around, he would sleep until about 4 am, then Dad would wake him up.

"Time to get up and kill that pig," Dad would say.

Bennie would roll out of bed, rub his eyes to get the sleep out, and head for the pen. Pigs were running all around – seemed like they knew one of them would not be sleeping there tonight.

Bennie would ask, "Which one, Dad?"

"That one." Daddy would point in the direction of a certain pig. Those pigs would still be running around the pen, but soon they would settle down. It was important to shoot that pig in the head, because any place else, and you could damage some good eating. It took a good marksman to get him on the first shot – right between the eyes – especially after a night of drinking.

So, Bennie would aim, slowly pulling the trigger and *bam*! The bullet went right through the head of that pig and he would flop over on the ground.

Right away, the neighbors who had come for the hog killing would gather 'round the carcass and put a sac they had soaked in boiling water on that now-dead pig. They would leave it there for a few minutes, and when they pulled that sac off, all the hair would come off, too. It was amazing how that worked!

Right after that, they would get Ira Hill to get ready for his part. He was a really, truly alcoholic. He would wake up with the shakes and couldn't get steady again until he had had his vodka. So, they would get him some vodka, and pretty soon he would be ready to cut the back legs of that pig.

He would go into that leg with the surgical precision like you'd see in the finest hospital in the world. He would reach inside with his pocketknife and pull out a "leader" that led all the way up the hog's leg.

Next, they would insert hooks into the legs and pull that old fat pig upside down over a branch in a certain tree and start the bleeding. We called that the hog killing tree.

Red blood would run like a river once it started. It would gather in puddles on the ground until the raging current would become a "slow flow". Then, once the bleeding had slowed down, the next step would be to begin to butcher it into its various wonderful cuts that made for good eating. The women got that job.

To this day, when I drive past that old tree, I see bloody puddles at its base. I hear the chatter of the women as they begin to cut all the various parts of that animal that will sustain us through part of the winter. I see the men, now that their work is pretty much done, begin their drinking. It's a real party.

The entire neighborhood would be there, helping and sharing. My dad would be at the helm...watching but not drinking, hearing but not swearing like the others, and being the deacon.

I always respected my dad, but on hog killing day especially. Our whole community shared the work and the benefits. We had a dinner right there when some of the parts were cooked, others were hung in the smoking shed, and some had gone directly to people's houses. Biscuits, gravy, and *fresh* pork like you can't have anyplace else, except at a hog killing.

Sometimes, though, my older brothers got the biggest portions, and there wasn't as much left for me as I would like. They were 9 and 12 when I was born – growing boys with huge appetites.

My oldest brother was Bennie, born in 1954. He was tough, and I can prove it: One day I wanted to ride one of our Shetland ponies, but Midnight wasn't interested in carrying me around.

She always knew how to behave when she saw Bennie come around; it had been a battle between two stubborn forces, and they had evidently had it out sometime before. Midnight would always act nice when he was there, so one day when I wanted to ride, Bennie came out, and I got on. Bennie just stood there in the yard and watched as I rode her around the house, in the yard and nearby, but then, Bennie went inside.

Uh oh.

Midnight got so mad, she ran down the road with me, and I couldn't jump off because I was on the hardtop. She just raced around like she was a wild one – all 400 pounds of her running up and down the road and going in circles.

Yes, I was scared. But then Bennie came out, and I was close enough to the ditch to jump off safely. Midnight ran into the Lockridge's yard, and it was there that Bennie caught up to her.

It was clear Bennie was fed up with Midnight's fooling around. He wasn't going to have any more of it. They danced around each other with the dirt flying as they each dug their heels in the ground and squared up.

He bent down, wrapped one arm just under Midnight's neck and lifted that horse up off the ground. I mean all four hooves had air under them! All 400 pounds of her!

Next thing you know Midnight was headed for the ground! He slam dunked that pony! THUD! The pony laid there for a minute, then kind of shook her head and slowly raised herself up on all fours.

I guess she was thinking "Game over, and Robert gets to ride any time he wants to." In fact, every other time I wanted to ride, I got it. No more hand-to-horse combat.

Bennie was built with good hard muscles and was used to hard work. He quit high school before graduation, though, and went to work at the local chicken factory.

Qunnie, she came next. She was born in 1956, sandwiched between Bennie and Larry, and a little of their "wild side" rubbed off on her. She was always respectful at home, but she made some questionable decisions outside the sight of the family.

For instance, in 1971 at the age of 15, she gave birth to her daughter, Daisy. And allegedly, she was involved in a bank robbery, but that has never been proved. There were just a few incidents where the family had to intervene to protect her. But she and Daisy have always been close to me, even to this day. Qunnie is a quiet person, and sometimes she has just a mysterious smile…kind of like the Mona Lisa. You never know what she is thinking.

Larry was brother number 2 – born in 1958 – and had a twin brother who did not survive the birthing process.

I think there's a thing called "survivor's guilt," a psychological explanation for why some folks have difficulty living when someone close to them dies. Well, Larry was the surviving twin.

Larry seemed like he was angry all his life. He didn't finish high school, either, and it seemed as soon as he could start drinking, he did. And he drank – hard drinking – all his life. He and Bennie would go out and party and come home drunk.

Some folks are happy drunks – they consume lots of alcohol and then go to sleep, but Larry wasn't that kind of drinker. He was the kind that the more he drank, the madder he got. And the madder he got, the more he wanted to fight – anybody he saw.

One time, he threatened to hit Momma. He didn't get far with that between Daddy and Bennie. Another time, when the two of them came in all drunken up, Daddy got up and gave them a talking to. Bennie was most respectful of his father, but Larry was just hard-headed and more belligerent. Finally, Daddy hauled off and hit him – HARD. I was so surprised that my daddy could do that… He laid Larry down on the floor with that blow.

Larry learned a lesson that night: just because Daddy was older didn't mean he would buckle down to his misbehaving boys. No, sir!

Bennie and Larry had a sideline business once they quit school. They would wait on a Friday until some cousins came in town. They would round up a load of guns and marijuana from the more rural areas in Mississippi, where the police had a hard time keeping the black market under control. Then Bennie and Larry would load them in their car and head to Detroit, where other cousins took over the "business." Then they would come on back and go to work at their jobs on Monday.

But Bennie always said, before they left on Friday night, "Robert, don't you do this, you hear? "Do as I say, not as I do! Don't you drink or do drugs!" I can hear him saying that to this day.

Then they'd head out, speeding toward Michigan.

One time, Bennie had messed up the payments or supply chain or something. All I know is there was a white car – a Ford four-door – in the parking lot of the church next door with several guys waiting outside. They stood in the shadows with their weapons visible, and periodically they lit cigarettes for each other. You could see small, orange spots glow brighter as they sucked in that gray smoke. It looked like about five orange circles, sometimes bright, sometimes dull, but moving around as the men paced nervously. They could be heard muttering amongst themselves – getting more and more impatient as time went on.

Their presence spoke fear. We all thought they planned to kill Bennie.

Inside the house, we were all scared… Daddy was still at work at the Purnell Pride chicken factory that night, and Momma, my sisters, my niece Daisy, me, Bennie, and Larry were huddled tightly together. I know I was *really* scared, and I wasn't alone. Momma finally said to Bennie, "You gotta go on outside there and take care of this situation."

He opened the door and walked into the darkness. As he moved closer to the men, those orange spots were ground into the pavement of the parking lot.

All of us kids were holding our breath. I think Momma was, too.

We didn't hear anything – no gunshots, no fighting, and soon they were gone, and Bennie came back in.

Smiling, he said to the gathered family, "I think the problem is solved. Funny how cousins in law enforcement can change the situation, isn't it?" He had just told those guys about one of our cousins that worked for one of the local police departments. They never came back again.

The drinking and carousing around caught up to Larry in the end, though. In 1987, when he was 29, he suffered a massive stroke and was paralyzed on the left side. He was wheelchair-bound for the rest of his life. He was even angrier, if that was possible, and he still wanted to drink and smoke. He was a sight to see – any weather, any day of the week, he would be hand wheeling that chair along the dusty side of the road, headed to the corner store to get some more cigarettes. Thirteen years of living like that and he had a second stroke. He never came home from the hospital after that one. Daisy said that while he was in the hospital, though, he had a turnaround and dedicated his life to Christ. He talked to Reverend Lewis Lockridge, and before the pastor left the hospital, Larry had raised his hand to the sky, as if in praise. A few days later, he suffered back-to-back seizures and died. He was 42.

Berta Mae, my second-oldest sister, was born in 1959 and was named after our full-blooded Choctaw grandmother. She went to Guntown School during the awful days of integration and has told me many times about her experiences and mistreatments in those days.

"Nigger, go home," echoed through the hallways. Once, a white boy spit on a black boy because the black boy could run faster than he could. Both were on the track team, but when the incident occurred, the black boy hit the spitter. He was suspended and couldn't run on the team. The white boy got no punishment and went on to win the race.

Berta felt hated during those years - so much so that she dropped out of high school during her junior year and got a job at the Natchez Trace Parkway Visitor's Center. She and Willie Ruff were married soon after and had three children, Willie Dante, Keith, and Stephanie.

Berta helped to raise me, and according to her, I always felt as though she was more than a big sister – not quite my momma, but pretty close. I am sure that I have some of her traits in my soul.

Berta and Ruff's house was my "second home," that's for sure. She would make my favorite meals any time of day. I could smell those pinto beans with pork roast, onions, potatoes, and carrots when I came through the door. Or maybe it would be pork chops with gravy and biscuits. Or anything chocolate. Breakfast, lunch, or dinner, there always seemed to be something good to eat when I came around. Even today, there still is!

She's always taken care of me, but there was one time I had to console her. Her son, Willie Dante, lived in a white neighborhood, and on the night after Thanksgiving in 2006, he was found dead at the door to his house. You would have thought I could have done something to help her – but I couldn't. It was the same time as when I was on suspension, and nobody paid any attention to me. There was a devil of a time getting an autopsy report; it took four years, and the authorities didn't want to even release any information about the incident at all. I didn't see the report, but I do know he was shot in the left side of the head. But he was right-handed, so it wasn't suicide. There was a letter in his mailbox addressed to the daughter of the Pontotoc County sheriff. That was another part of the mystery that was never revealed to this day.

I also remind you, this was not only the Thanksgiving after the Allan case, it was at the height of the legal issues against me.

There has never been a resolution to his murder.

Berta was heartbroken, but all I could do was hold on to her and let her cry.

The last of the sisters to be born was Diane, who was born two years after Berta. As far as Momma knew, that was her last baby.

Diane liked to hide from Momma and Daddy and eat sugar straight from the bag. She would also hold it in her hand to feed the horse.

In 1966, when she was 5, the family moved from the Patterson homestead to Saltillo, where we took care of Momma's Uncle Albert until he died. Memories fade, but Diane remembers playing outside with all the younger siblings, being spoiled, and going with me every year to cut down a Christmas tree and make the stand to hold it with a bucket of mud and rocks. She has three children: Johnathan, Courtney, and Avita. I used to babysit Johnathan before he left for college. She always felt we were lucky to be spoiled. Maybe being the last two, we did get special treatment.

If I'm talking about my siblings, I only have five but in truth, I have an "almost sister" in Daisy, Qunnie's daughter. She was the first grandchild in the family and was born in 1971. We were so close growing up. Sometimes at night, she would have to go out to the outhouse after everyone was asleep. It fell to me to escort her out there…in the dark of night with owls hooting, and there was no telling what other critters could be out there if you're five or six years old. She held tight to me, turning her head back and forth and shivering, even on summer nights. Her imagination went wild as she described the bad things she feared – monsters who would snatch her up and whisk her away, snakes that could wrap themselves around you and squeeze you to death. Animals that were giants and would maybe eat her up. She would climb up the steps and open the door. As she turned around to sit down, she would make me promise not to leave her. "You hear me, Robert? Don't you leave me to those monsters." And while she did her business, I'd wait outside the door.

One time, she told Diane and me that she was going to run away. She packed a jug of water and her school clothes, but after a while, she changed her mind.

She was a perfect little sister. And still is.

That's all my own generation, and there is a world of difference between Bennie, a child of the early '50s and me, born twelve years later.

Another very consistent element in my young life was church.

I know that who I am was shaped not only by my family and neighborhood and friends, but also by the church we attended. I still attend that same church to this day.

It is a "family" church. Even though it was a neighborhood church, and the largest in the area, it was populated mostly by folks who were related to

The Hall family, circa 1980
First row (L to R): B.T., Florine (holding Avita), Stephanie, Kenneth, Keith, Johnathan Demitrius, Willie Dante
Second row (L to R): Robert, Berta Mae, Bennie (holding Courtney), Daisy

me. In those days and times, sisters, brothers, mothers, fathers, aunts, uncles, cousins, and grandparents all seemed to live within shouting distance of each other. So, it made sense that we all went to the same church.

I can't remember my first time at church because it was so central to our everyday life. We went to church *every* Sunday, rain, shine, snow, or sleet.

Well, there was *one* day when we missed.

As I said, Dad was a deacon. He also was very particular about being there *on time*! This one Sunday, he was ready, and Momma wasn't. She was putting on her lipstick and other such makeup, and Dad got impatient.

"If you aren't ready in five minutes, I'm going, and I'm driving myself!" he shouted. Now, he couldn't drive a lick, and Momma knew he couldn't drive, so she didn't think he would dare to try.

Well, he did. He went out and got in the car. He put the key in the starter place and pressed his foot to the gas...hard. Remember, he was only used to driving a wagon pulled by a mule or a horse – and it was slow. So, when he hit the gas pedal, that car shot over across the road into a neighbor's fence and stopped. Dad put it in gear, got it out of the ditch, and drove on down the highway, weaving and fishtailing all the way to church.

Momma and us kids stayed at home that day. And Daddy drove to church and back.

But that's the only day Momma wasn't ready, and we always made it on time after that.

We were all dressed up, too. As I said earlier, Bennie and Larry were often out drinking and carousing around and would come home in the wee hours of the morning. But no matter: they had to get up and wear their crumpled, smelly clothes to church. The rest of us were clean, pressed, and smelling good. *Nothing* interfered with going to church.

Church was simply non-negotiable when we were children. When Larry got to be an adult, he didn't care for church, so he quit going.

Bennie faithfully attended into adulthood, until he observed two deacons at church having a confrontation in church. They took the fight outside, and one drew a knife and slit the other. That soured Bennie on going to church. If deacons would behave like that, he didn't see the reason to attend. Later in life though, he found God and made amends, but he never did go through the doors of church again.

Black church services often last from 11 in the morning (after Sunday School, which starts at 9) until around 1 in the afternoon. In the old days, some church families would eat on the grounds and socialize until it was time for the evening service. Sunday was Church Day.

Daddy was a deacon in the church, and I so admired him. He took care of folks in his family, and he doted on his wife, but he took care of people in his church, too. I wanted to be just like him.

One of Dad's brothers had moved to St. Louis where, among other things he did, he was a preacher. He never forgot his roots, and he would often return in the hot summers of Mississippi to run a revival.

Oh, when he came to town, the church would be full as a tick. Gospel songs like "Bur-don Down", and "I Wanna Live So God Can Use Me" would rattle the rafters, and everyone would celebrate the Lord.

That was the only place where black folks could be free; we could sing until tears ran down everyone's face. We would pray for several minutes at a time, just pouring it on.

Both adults and kids were present in the church, though children sat on the "mourners" bench. That bench was reserved for people who had not yet been baptized. At some time in their lives, they would accept Jesus as their Savior, and they would then be baptized. But until then, they sat on that bench.

All the folks would be singing and clapping and shouting. It was like getting ready for a ballgame – cheerleaders got the group ready, the singers and prayer leaders set the stage for the preacher, and the preacher would bring the Word.

Once my uncle from St. Louis got up, it was almost like President Obama had come to visit. He took it to the house. People would be on their feet, clapping, witnessing to what he was saying. "Come on, Preacher!"

At the end, he would give the invitation to all, but especially to the sinners on the bench. They would become saved at some time. There was no particular age when we had to go up – just when we felt it was time. No one pushed us, and that stood for older "sinners", too.

One of the most memorable events in my young life was the day they called me up.

I was about 12 and sitting on the "mourners" bench when the men of the church reached out their hands, urging me to come to the altar. "Come on up and get this done."

That day, I eased off the bench. They thought I was trying to figure out if God was real, but I was trying to decide if it was the time in the ceremony for me to do this.

I heard them call my name, and I responded. I rose and headed to the altar area. The Lord was calling me to the church.

I always say we were so poor we couldn't afford the second "o" in the word. "Poor" means your kids have fat stomachs because there is not enough food, and lots of the kids die before they even get to go to school.

To me, "rich" doesn't just mean you have lots of money. "Rich" means folks love you; they take care of you and make you laugh. They are always there to protect you.

I was raised "rich."

Chapter Two

How Did I Get in This Spot?

All my troubles began because I was a cop – and a black cop in a Southern state to boot. I was a black cop in a state that has a long history of mistreatment of blacks from whites.

Now, don't get me wrong. I know all whites aren't abusive to black folks. But there are still a lot of them sneaking around the state, even today.

Nobody forced me to be in law enforcement. No, I wanted that from the get-go. I had been riding in squad cars since I was a child. I was born after segregation ended, and the local police department had put a token number of blacks on the force. Those guys were way ahead of their time; they were doing "community policing". They were reaching out to neighborhood folks to build relationships with those citizens so they could protect and serve those people when needed. It was what they did – befriend all ages of folks in their territory.

When I was kid, my older uncles or cousins who were in law enforcement would ask if I wanted to ride in the squad car, and I would jump in the car in a flash and shout, "Yes!"

Herman Hill, Ira Hill's son, was in the sheriff's office across the street from the Tupelo Police Department. When I was older, his nephew Anthony Hill and I got uniforms. They were unofficial, but we didn't care. We proudly wore our khaki pants and a shirt with an official-looking emblem designating us as Junior Police Auxiliary.

We both thought we were some kind of superior. We got to go to the jail or the police department or sit in the dispatcher's office and see what was going on in the county areas we knew.

"Did you see what's going on in Saltillo?" I'd ask, and Anthony would nod his head wisely. "Over east of town, some guy was speeding, did you see that?" he'd ask. "Sure did," I'd reply.

Those were the good old days when we were "play cops". Riding in the squad car was fun. We would sometimes go fast, sometimes slowly cruise around the neighborhoods. Herman would roll down the window and yell out to somebody, "Hey, there, Moses! How's the wife?"

That's how you build relationships. You know the kids, you know the wife, and you recognize if something is out of order in their front yard. "You need help getting that junk taken to the back yard?"

Sometimes, there were real cop jobs to be done. I had my first real cop experience when I was about ten years old.

Two of my classmates from school turned up missing. It was summertime, and we were all out of school with nothing to do and nowhere to go.

Huzzie and Gertie were a brother and sister that lived a bicycle ride away from my own home, but in an area that my neighbor, Mr. Burt wouldn't let me ride into. Mr. Burt was part of my "neighborhood of parents" – folks who looked out for all the kids in our area.

Rumor was that there were "bad things" going on up at Huzzie and Gurtie's so I stayed away. I only saw them at school.

That time, nobody had seen them for a couple of days, and their momma was almost crazy. She was crying sometimes and screaming sometimes and sometimes just shaking her head and wringing her hands.

All the parents in the area, plus others, were all over the land, through the fields, in the woods, checking the houses and buildings front and back. They were carrying sticks and swatting at the tall grasses. They were all calling at the top of their lungs, "Huzzie! Gertie! Gertie! Huzzie!" At night, they had flashlights, but they still kept walking that land.

One evening, I'd been riding with Sheriff Herring while all the other folks were searching for them. He let me out not far from my house, which was kind of close to Mr. Burt's house. Mr. Burt was standing in his yard, and since he was my friend, I ambled over toward him as the sheriff drove off.

Now, Mr. Burt was a neighbor, and we rode together a lot – he even taught me how to drive a pickup. Sometimes I hung around his house, even when he wasn't home, just swinging on his front porch. We were close.

But as I walked toward him, I saw Mr. Burt had a funny look on his face. He didn't even see me coming toward him or hear my greeting.

He was looking at his big old chest freezer he had in his yard. I followed him with my hands in my pockets as he headed toward that long, white box sitting under the tree.

Something wasn't right. He reached over and opened that freezer.

He didn't say anything, and I didn't say anything.

He looked like he was frozen himself.

I strode up to him as he stood there, transfixed – hypnotized.

I get chills when I think of it.

As I peered over the edge of the freezer, there were my two friends, Huzzie and Gertie, with their dog in between them.

They looked just like they could jump out of there, and I wondered, "Huzzie? Gertie? Why are you in there? Come on out!" They didn't move, and there were bubbles running out of their noses and mouths.

Mr. Burt looked so shocked. Like he couldn't believe what he saw.

I quickly took off running to my house.

"Momma, Momma! They found Huzzie and Gertie! They're in Mr. Burt's freezer!"

After that, chaos broke loose. Everybody ran to the freezer. Cop cars with sirens came screaming down the road to Mr. Burt's house, and an ambulance arrived, too.

All the searchers came in from the fields and from the woods and everywhere they had been yelling for the kids.

"How'd that happen? Why were they in there? How long do you think they've been there? Did you see the dog was there with them?"

'Course, no one thought Mr. Burt had murdered them. They knew better. Huzzie and Gertie's home life had been so chaotic, to say the least. After all, that was why Mr. Burt didn't let me ride my bike down there.

They may have been playing hide and seek, or they may have been hiding from what was going on at their house. No one knows.

No one will ever know.

I ached for Huzzie and Gertie. I wanted to be able to help them, but they were beyond help.

Their deaths weren't real to me until the funeral. I kept thinking they would somehow be back in school soon.

But at the funeral, the church was filled to the brim. Sniffles were heard all over the room, and their momma just sobbed and sobbed. There they lay, both dressed in good clothes, but sleeping. Seemed like the dog should be there, too. Their momma cried so hard and hugged Huzzie so hard, I thought she was going to get him out of that casket and take him home. That's when I knew they were dead.

Today, freezers and such are built with an escape mechanism so no one can get locked inside and suffocate like they did.

About two years ago, I stopped in to see their mom. When you walk in the front door, the first thing you see are their last family pictures, with everybody smiling as though it was Christmas or something. There they are, frozen in time – ten years old forever.

A year or so after Huzzie and Gertie died, I woke up in the night with lights flashing on the walls of our house. Everyone seemed to get up at about the same time, and Daddy and I ran out of the house to find a trailer down the road from us was on fire.

All the neighbors stood in the shadows of a fire that was engulfing an entire dwelling. I remember feeling the heat of the blaze, hearing the voices of the kids trapped inside screaming, and the most unbelievable sense of emptiness I've ever known.

How can I describe an inferno that will kill six children so you can feel the pain?

Firemen say a fire is a living entity. You can see it breathe – the blaze goes in and out like you or me when we inhale and exhale. And that description fits.

Can you hear the groan of the trailer as the fire consumes its wood 2x4s? Do you hear the sizzle and pop as various pieces of glass and moisture are consumed by the blazes? Or can you hear the constant "fwoom" or "whoosh" of the flames? Sometimes that same fire sounds like the crunching of leaves only it never stops – until the fire is out.

Against the dark of the night sky, the entire area was so bright you could read the paper if you wanted to. These blazes licked at the sky with a ferocity that is hard to imagine if you've never seen it. And in an instant, the trailer and my friends were gone. Before we knew it, Kenneth Young, 10 years old; Ann Young, 6 years old; Charoyale Young, 3 years old; and three other children were dead. I would never see their laughing faces again, not as neighbors or as school mates. And the place where the trailer used to be was just a flat pile of debris. There were no beams, nothing.

It was simply ashes on the ground.

As the dawn began to peek through the trees and the air cooled a bit as the fire abated, we saw a horrifying sight.

Six skeletons lay among the ashes. My friends had no flesh on their bodies. They were just a framework of bones.

One of the older children seemed to have been holding a baby in her arms. I guess they were trying to get out the door, but the smoke or flames got them first. Then the blazes just ate them all up, except for their bones.

We all stood there in silence.

You might think these things are lost in the mists of time, but when I showed this manuscript to a friend, she fell into tears. "I was related to those children. I never thought anyone else would remember them."

I can't really explain how deeply those two events affected me. Somehow, I knew those people had needed help and we – me, my family, the neighbors, and the local police – were all trying to ease the pain. But we couldn't.

More than that, these deaths of my friends at such a young age impacted me more than I can tell.

Without really understanding why, at that moment I knew I wanted to be like my friends who were policemen. I wanted to be in a career where I could help the elderly and kids and anyone else in trouble. I wanted to be a cop.

Robert, circa 1980, on the Saltillo Tigers football team

Chapter Three

BFF, NECC and I'm a Working Man

My best friend in school was Rod Cobb. He moved to Saltillo from Union County in the ninth grade, and we became best friends forever.

We talked a lot about a lot of things, as boys do. Mostly we discussed our futures. What kind of a woman we wanted to marry (she had to be a good Christian woman who belonged to a church). What we would do for a living. Of course, we also ran through the football games from the past weekend, too.

One day when we were about seventeen, Rod asked me what college I was going to.

"College?" I asked. "What do you mean?"

"I'm going to Northeast Community College in Booneville," he said. "Where are you going?"

Now, Rod was from a different world than me. His parents both had college degrees and taught in public schools. They drove up north and went on vacations every year. His parents wanted their two boys to see the rest of the country, so he had seen cities like St. Louis, Detroit, and Chicago. *And* they lived in a brick house. His world was different, but we were the best of friends.

There was nobody in my family that had even graduated from high school, much less gone to a college!

Rod kept on. "You can get a scholarship over there for your athletic skills. You are so good at football and basketball, you could go and have it already paid for!"

He may as well have been speaking Russian or Chinese to me. My family didn't go to college. We were workers – in factories, on farms. We didn't do much "book learning" that I knew of.

But I must admit, the idea of going to college to play ball was attractive. What else would I do after graduating? At least Rod was headed there, so I wouldn't be alone, and he had been my best friend for the past four years. And, I have to admit, I did envy his lifestyle.

His mom and dad, who were both teachers, pitched in and helped me apply, and lo and behold, I was accepted!

We graduated from high school, and before I knew it, it was time to head off to Booneville, Mississippi, for my first days at college.

Me! Going to college.

The summer went by in a flash, and we were off to college.

Just before we were to move in, Rod asked me, "Are you going to be in a dorm at NECC?".

"I don't know," I replied. I had not thought that far ahead. Dorm? I didn't have money for things like that.

By then, there were no rooms available at the college, and my family didn't have the money for a dorm anyway. Rod's folks were rich compared to us.

So, my family got together and began to think what to do. So we sat down after dinner one night in the kitchen.

"We got to get Robert to NECC," Daddy said. "I can't drive him, because I'll be at work. Bennie, can you take him on your way to work?"

Bennie and Tommy Richey (Qunnie's cousin) were working at a furniture factory near Booneville, so I could ride with them to and from school.

Only one problem: they had to be at work at 6 am. That was one early commute!

So fall term, Rod came to my rescue. When my brother and cousin dropped me off, Rod would come down from his dorm room, unlock the door, and let me in. Then I would snooze until my first class.

You can imagine two college freshmen at 5:30 am in the morning – Rod slugging down the stairs to open the door to me, equally sleepy. Neither one of us were "morning people" at that time.

But we made it through the first semester.

My major was social work. Don't quite know how I got that, but when I registered, they asked me what I wanted to do.

"I want to help people," I said, and that's where they put me. One semester of that and I knew it wasn't for me.

When I walked into class the first time, I was struck by the fact that my classmates were almost all women! I wanted a masculine career.

And secondly, you had to sit at a desk most of the time. That was not me! I like to be moving around, out in the town, meeting people, not locked in an office.

So after the first semester, I got good enough grades and Dad had saved up enough money that I could get a room and only go home on the weekends. That meant I got to sleep a lot longer in the mornings.

My second semester went a bit better. I changed to a criminal justice major. I should have been there from the start. I really wanted to be in law enforcement. I'd been a "kid cop" already. I just needed to take the next step.

And there were more men in my classes, and I knew I wouldn't spend my days behind a desk.

But the best thing was that Daddy bought me a 1972 Pontiac Catalina for $400 – a blue car with a white top! The kids at college called it my "blue box," but I didn't care. I had my own car!

Daddy had also roamed the roads near our house to gather cans so he could help with expenses: gas, snacks, and maybe even some date money. My dad, walking the roads after he retired so he could get money for his son to go to college. I am humbled when I close my eyes and see that image in my mind.

When I think of those days at Northeast, I realize how limited my life had been. The other students there, like Rod, were heading off after graduation, going to the universities in the state. He was an architecture major heading for Mississippi State University in Starkville. I wasn't headed anywhere that I knew of.

Whatever I did there, whether it was play basketball or sit in my classes, I never felt like I fit in. Rod was not athletic, but he was academic, and he did fit in. He never tried to make me feel out of place, but I just did.

I was poorer, dressed in only two outfits per week, and borrowed Rod's shoes to play basketball in. I didn't have any plans for going to Mississippi State or Ole Miss. I was just sort of a fish out of water.

I never really felt like I fit there, but I am so grateful for the experience.

My third semester came around in the fall of 1986, and I thought I was set to finish in the near future. I liked my major in criminal justice, and I loved the psychology classes best of all – though my public speaking class gave me a really good foundation for the future. I went from a stumbling, bumbling idiot in front of a crowd to comfortably talking to large groups of people. I needed that.

I thought life was planned out for me. But God had a different plan in mind.

One day, I got a call at the dorm that I needed to call the hospital in Tupelo.

The message was bad: Daddy was really sick, and I needed to get there.

I jumped in my little car and drove like a bat out of Hell to get home. I had to pick up Larry, and together, we needed to head to the hospital.

When I got home, Larry was drunk – no surprise. I tried to get him into the car, but he was hard to handle.

"We've got to hurry. Daddy's bad off."

Larry wouldn't be hurried. "He's gone, you know… He's gone, so no need to race."

By the time we got there, Daddy had passed.

The Hall family, circa 1990
Front row (left to right): Berta Mae, Larry, Florine
Second row (left to right): Diane, Qunnie, Robert, Bennie

Momma and Uncle Early, Daddy's brother, were in the room with his body, but I didn't want to go in. I don't know if it was fear or disbelief, but I didn't want to see him in that state.

I saw him first in the casket, and I recognized one of my ties around his neck. I stood there for the funeral, but I didn't go to the cemetery. I was not yet 19 years old, and I couldn't imagine this strong, spiritual, caring, energetic man who had fathered six children lying there dead in the casket. It wasn't real.

In the aftermath of his death, I tried to return to college, but I missed the gas money and extra cash he had gathered up for me by the roadsides.

Momma was feeling the tighter budget, too. She was getting only his Social Security check instead of his salary and other income he used to contribute to help keep the household running. The writing on the wall was clear. I would have to quit school and get a job. None of my siblings were able to help, so I dropped out of Northeast and went to work.

That fall, I got a job at the Executive Inn in Tupelo. I was a bellman and banquet setup manager. I liked working there, though I knew I wasn't going to make a career of it. But it was a good transitional place until I got my feet on the ground.

As a bellman, I simply took the luggage to the rooms for folks who were staying over and ran errands for them and for the administrators of the hotel. My job as banquet setup manager meant I was responsible for dinners, conferences, and getting the rooms ready for the meetings. I liked both of those roles because I enjoyed meeting people and chatting with them, and I liked helping people.

Among the "regulars" that frequented the hotel were a group of police officers. They might order lunch or maybe just a snack while relaxing and chatting. They looked like people who were happy in their jobs to me.

I knew that hotel work wasn't what I wanted for a lifetime career, so one day when the policemen came in, I decided I'd ask them about being an officer of the police force.

"Excuse me, I've got a question for you. I think I'd like to be a policeman. What would I do to get a job there?"

Northeast Community College criminal justice majors, 1984
Robert on front row at left end

They smiled and told me that all I had to do was check with the Tupelo Police Department. *Easy enough.* I decided that was something I'd do.

Would you believe that the very day that I approached the policemen, I saw an ad in the *Northeast Mississippi Daily Journal* saying there were openings in the police force? I just had to check at headquarters about taking the exam. I called and got hold of the right person.

"We'd be happy to talk to you, young man. But first you will have to take a test. We will send you the paperwork. Good luck".

Within a few days, a letter with the date of the test and an invitation to participate arrived.

I told my cousin Herman Hill, the policeman, about it. He was bound and determined to help me. So a day or so later, I met him out at his house, and he taught me how to take the test.

He got comfortable in his easy chair and looked me in the eye for a minute or so without speaking. Then he said, "Tests are structured to focus on common sense. When they ask you if you want to go to a bank robbery or help an old lady, you say help the old lady. Most others would say 'Go to the bank robbery,' because they think that's the exciting place to be. No one should want to shoot or kill people. They should always want to help people. Especially children and old folks."

He ended with a sage piece of advice. "You want to be a normal person using common sense."

I followed his advice when I went to take the exam. That day, the applicants included me and another 60 or so people, most of whom were white. We were all nervous, shaking on the inside and trying to look calm on the outside. I must have done well, because I received a call to come in and interview with Chief Ed Crider.

I made an appointment.

I dressed carefully so as to make a good impression. My shoes were shined, and I wore my "rat tail" hair, figuring I looked really cool.

I walked into the headquarters, and Chief Crider jumped up from his chair, shook my hand, and began questioning me.

Those early questions sounded exactly like what my uncle had warned me about, and I tried to sound like I was using common sense. Then he said, "How would you treat a drunk if you were on the street and had to bring him into jail?"

I thought and answered, "I guess, sir, like I would want to be treated if I were drunk."

He said, "That is exactly what I wanted to hear." Then, he leaned back in his chair and took a long look at me.

He said, "You look just like a good friend of mine that died. I'm going to hire you."

So now, my dreams had come true – ever since I was a kid, I'd wanted to be a policeman, and now I was going to wear the uniform and help those who could not help themselves.

I was going to be a cop.

Chapter Four

Rookie and Dispatcher

I was hired just before my 21st birthday, and I was too young to go to the police academy. The question then was what to do with me between the day I was hired and the day I started at the academy (which was, incidentally, the day after my 21st birthday).

I went in that morning full of pride. I had my uniform on, my gun was on my belt, and I was ready. I thought I would be riding in a patrol car like I had done as a younger kid, but this time I would be a full-time, real cop.

The shift captain entered the meeting room and began reading the patrolling assignments for the day. "So-and-So with So-and-So," "John Smith with Lou Doe," and so on and so on.

I anxiously awaited my turn.

Pretty soon, I was the only one left without an assignment.

"Sir, where am I going to be?" I asked.

Now, our captain fancied himself as quite a comic. "You've got the biggest radio of all, son! You are the dispatcher! You control all the areas today." And he repeated, "You are the dispatcher."

Now, my heart was pounding. I'm sure my face showed my disappointment. Dispatcher wasn't what I wanted to be. The rest of the folks were out on the streets, patrolling where the action was. I sure didn't want to be sitting in the office!

I felt like I'd been kicked in the gut. Here I was, almost 21 years old, armed with a government-issue gun and a professional looking uniform, and I was going to be sitting in a tiny glass cubicle in a windowless room? I sat at a big desk, dwarfed by a huge, ancient radio set, an equally ancient computer, and log books, logging every call that came in and went out.

I decided to look on the bright side. I would do this job better than anybody else had ever done it.

The dispatcher *did* control the whole city. Tupelo is a two-railroad town, and the layouts of those towns are distinctive; they grow up around the tracks. The tracks run through the very center of town, where the main roads intersect. Traffic jams often occur due to the lumbering multi-car transports that beat a constant rhythm as they cross the ties on the rails. Click-a-drum. Click-a-drum. Click-a-drum. Young children used to wait eagerly for that last car, a red caboose, to come into sight. Often an employee would be sitting by the open window and would wave to the kids.

It was always a joy for waiting drivers to see the end of those freight cars emerge from the curves. They shoved their sedans, SUVs, vans, or trucks into gear and began to move again. These people were going who knows where to do who knows what, but they were always in a hurry. It's the pulse of a small city – the heartbeat that keeps that urban body alive.

Our town is a pretty normal town, except it's been named an All-American City multiple times now. We aren't the cotton plantation owners, slave holders, or wealthy folks of the Delta; no, we are small acreage farmers. The soil is, admittedly, just ordinary, but we are an area that has made its fame in dairy farming and manufacturing. It's on the tail end of the Appalachian Mountain chain, which means we qualify for some federal grant money and have a few rolling hills.

You can see the sky and the clouds over the fields from most of the roads around here, but once you head into Tupelo proper, it becomes a small city. We have our mall, and the eight-screen Cinemark theater brings the latest films to this end of the state. We aren't a fancy metropolitan place, but we are more than a wide spot in the road between Memphis, Tennessee and Birmingham, Alabama. Toyota thought enough of us to build a Corolla plant nearby. Their employees number 2,000 or so folks. Ancillary businesses add to our local workforce, and the workers in all those companies usually shop in downtown Tupelo.

We don't have many murders, but we do have domestic violence and a fair number of robberies. We are a pretty safe place to live, if I do say so myself.

I took calls from the hospital, the ambulance, and the fire department, as well as the police department. I would come to know every street, neighborhood, business, school, church, and home in the city. Before long, I was able to send the officers to an area where they would be most effective.

Black officers called me "rookette" instead of "rookie," and the white guys on the force called me "boy," but either way it meant the same – I was a newbie and at the bottom of the ladder.

I would sit there, enclosed in that glass cage. Cops would come in off their shift and pace back and forth while teasing me unmercifully. They learned that they'd better be careful though, because when I had to go to lunch, someone had to sit in for me, and I got to pick who.

Most of the cops hated to do dispatch, but no one more so than Marion Morrow. He was heavyset at 340 pounds and didn't really fit in the chair. He also had a speech impediment, which often made it hard for the other officers to understand him. I usually waited until he wasn't busy, then would call him in to take over for me."Nine-un-un," he would say when the phone rang. We became very good friends, and when I did get the chance to ride in the car with a more experienced officer, I rode with him.

Marvin Brown was another one of the officers I came to know working at dispatch. He was the training officer, but he couldn't read or write. He taught me the streets, and I helped him by writing his reports.

One night, a lady called in. She said her husband was beating her and that he had a gun and a knife. Now, domestic violence calls are among the most dangerous calls police handle. They would always take two men, and they had to fully understand the situation. For instance, it might not be wise to go breaking through the door. This particular man was really violent and was armed.

I had picked three cops for this call: Marion Marrow, who was not in the best of health; "Cotton" Jimmy McCoy; and Bobby Mann (who considered himself "sugar turned into shit"). He was always looking for a good fight.

Well, Cotton and Mann arrived, and I moved Marion to the back yard of the house.

Now, that arrogant, abusive, and likely drunk husband was lying on the couch when they got there. He was talking on the phone with someone and whistling like he was in a musical.

Marion could see that if you came through the front door, you could catch him by surprise. He was not in the kitchen, where the knife was on the table.

His wife had told me the key to the house was hidden in the front, so Cotton and Bobby located it and quietly unlocked the door. They were able to call his name, and as he struggled to get off the couch, Bobby Mann quickly got him down.

"Got the gun – got the knife." I heard them breathing hard on the radio. "Had a firearm and knife, and victim is safe."

When they got back to the station, Bobby Mann strutted in with Cotton, their chests puffed out. They told me in unison, "We got 'em, Bobby."

Standing nearby, Shift Captain Larry Presley had the ever-present cigar in his mouth. Pulling it out, he simply said, "Well, I reckon that was a pretty good job."

My days of initiation to the force were many and frequent, but later in the summer, I stopped being just a rookie on the force and became one of the guys.

When the police are out on patrol, who's left in the station? The dispatcher and the jailer.

I found myself working a late shift on dispatch one night. It was 1:30 a.m., and the jailer was asleep. Suddenly, I heard a commotion in the jail. There were about 100 or more prisoners there that night, and I could hear chanting.

"Fight, fight! They are killing each other here!"

It was up to 20-year-old, 135-pound me to get help so we didn't have a riot.

Knowing that the jailer was a civilian and not a trained officer, I hesitantly woke him up. "Can you go over there and stop that?" I asked.

"Hell no!", he said. "I'm not going to go in that jail to stop a fight!"

I had to think fast. It was 1:30 at night, and the clubs were rocking. I knew the officers loved to go to those places, but there was so much noise, they couldn't hear their radios or the microphone.

I also knew that Marvin Brown got out and ate at the Waffle House about that time, and a female officer (among the first two women on the force) didn't like to get into those bars, so she was nowhere in sight.

I was on the radio looking for officers. I saw Bobby Mann's name listed as "on duty" and radioed him.

"Well", he asked, "is there trouble at 1062?" (That was the code for the station house.) I told him there was, he responded, "Hold on there, dispatch. I'll be there and take care of it."

Now, I had seen men who tried to fight with Bobby end up at the hospital. I was glad I had Bobby on my side.

He came back to the station, and he took care of the fight. No questions asked.

Things are different now. Rookies don't serve time as dispatchers, and I think that's a shame. That's how you learn the city. Today, there are at least four people in the station at one time working 911 and looking at all the screens. They do run the city, and if you don't have a good dispatcher, you're just hanging out there.

I spent about three or four months working that dispatch job before I turned 21 and went to the academy. I learned a great deal in that time. My experience ranged from writing the log of every call, including when they came in and went out, to answering the phones for the fire department, police, and ambulances. *And* I learned the streets and neighborhoods of the city. It was a busy job.

Rookies probably need to serve at the bottom of the ladder there, too. One night, on a Friday night with a full moon, I parked my brand-new

Nissan car in the parking lot and had just gotten in for my shift when a call came in from Cotton.

"I am in pursuit of a black car on McCulloch – got sirens going." He called in the tag number. I plugged it into the state database.

While I was typing, I heard Cotton say "I'll get close. Uh oh! He's just flipped it!"

The database pulled up the tag number, and I realized something. "Hell, that's my car!" I yelled.

I jumped up and ran out to the parking lot to where my car was – and there it sat, quiet and safe. The rank and file cops on duty had put one over on me.

I guess it takes a little while for us rookies to be initiated into the "brotherhood" of policemen, but once they accept you, you know that they have your back anytime, anywhere, under any circumstances, you are brothers.

I was one of them.

At the Mississippi Law Enforcement Officers Training Academy in Pearl, Mississippi, 1987

Chapter Five

At the Academy

It was a sunny day in September 1987. I was 21 years and one day old – legal for just about everything. My buddies Cliff Hardy and Tyrone Ashby met me at the police garage, and we picked up our car to drive to the academy in Pearl. We were heading south to be trained for our new jobs as police officers in the city of Tupelo, Mississippi.

They had been hired about the same time as I was, but Cliff was 27, so he had been able to ride with a patrolman until time came to go to the academy. Tyrone was the civilian dispatcher who shared my cubicle, watching screens alongside me.

Life was good, that's all.... Life was just good.

The highway stretched out before us. Bright blue sky and ribbons of concrete with wide medians of grass or trees in the middle. As we drove, we felt a freedom that only the young can feel. No real responsibilities...just a world full of possibilities ahead of us.

That sense of freedom caused Cliff to want to see how fast that big old white Buick they gave us from the department garage would go.

Now, Cliff likes to go fast, so he pressed the pedal to the metal and off we went.

Breezes and bugs hit the windshield. We were flying like the birds. Soaring south like eagles!

As you might imagine, it wasn't long before a shrieking siren showed up in the rearview mirror and blue lights flashed behind us.

Uh oh.

Here we were, going to learn to be policemen so we could catch speeders, and bingo – we got caught.

The Natchez Trace ranger slowly walked up to the car. He bent down and peered inside the car. There we sat in our starched and pressed Tupelo Police Department uniforms. "Where in hell are the three of you going at that speed?" he asked in a stern voice. We told him we were headed for the police academy in Pearl. Then he began to really read Cliff the Riot Act.

"What kind of a cop are you going to be? Huh? The kind that says, 'Do as I say and not as I do'? The kind that causes accidents instead of cleaning them up? Are you going to be the cops that cause more trouble than the average citizen can imagine?

"Get yourself under control, boys! You can't be speeding at such a rate on this highway where the limit is 50 miles an hour. The very fastest you could go is 62 miles per hour. Don't you ever go beyond that, you hear?"

After Cliff got chewed out for his speeding, I took over driving, and nearly three hours later, we arrived at Pearl, Mississippi, where the academy was. We disembarked from that old beat-up Buick and took our first steps toward becoming certified police officers.

The police academy at Pearl was the only one in the state when I enrolled in 1987. They taught all the law enforcement groups – Highway Patrol, city police, county sheriffs, game wardens – all the folks from the Gulf Coast to De Soto County, from the Mississippi River to the Alabama line and everything in between. Since then, more regional academies have opened, and it's a good thing, too. There's a whole lot more to teach since 1987.

Today's program deals with more technology, DNA, chemical weaponry, etc. than it did when I went there. It's longer, too. Today's officers will be there for twelve weeks, as opposed to the nine when I went. And today, the cost of that program is in the $4,000 range.

I'm glad I don't have to go now.

So, we appeared at the gates to the academy in Pearl, September 27, 1987.

Arrival day was "organizational." You got your uniform and gear and made sure you had all your stuff together. We learned how to make our beds – after you tucked the sheet at that certain angle, you had a six-inch collar, that part of the sheet showing under the spread. You used a dollar bill to measure that.

And we had to learn to salute. There is a proper way to do it, and you'd better stand straight like you've got a ramrod up your back. As you salute, your arm must be at a 90-degree angle; the tip of your fingers will touch your hat at your eyebrows. As to your uniform, your belt buckle must line up with the buttons on your shirt. If these things aren't right, you can just get ready to drop for push ups right then and there.

I had to learn to shine shoes (though I thought I already knew how to do that) – the *extra shiny* way. Like the military did. Cliff was a veteran, so he knew exactly how to shine those shoes to pass inspection. He made his shoes "shine like a Hershey bar!" he said.

What you do is this: put a little water inside the polish can and do a "first rub". Sprinkle it with water again and get you a cigarette lighter. Light that thing up and warm the polish up… then put it on your shoe and apply plain old elbow grease to the leather. Cliff saved Tyrone and me from embarrassment, extra push ups, and being chewed out in front of everyone there. I was grateful for that!

Monday morning was the very beginning of our training. We were a class of candidates from all over the state.

What I really liked about that was that I met folks from all over Mississippi: guys from the Coast, from the Delta, from the Prairie area, and of course, my guys from Tupelo. There were fifty of us in the group that September, and I can tell you that the friendships forged during our training have stood the test of time. Here we are thirty-five years on, and we still keep in touch. Sometimes it's professional, sometimes it's just friendship, but we keep in touch.

What you learn at the academy is basic stuff: how to drive fast, what to notice after a crime, and a myriad number of other things.

It was nine weeks of classroom lectures, field work, physical exercise to be sure we were fit, shooting exercises to be sure we know how to use the weapons, basic law enforcement courses, understanding of the laws that would apply to our street crimes, and psychology analysis.

It was comprehensive, but I will tell you that you get your education when you are on the street. There is no substitute for interactions with a situation, whether it be robbery, domestic violence, traffic accident – whatever. You learn your craft on the job.

I was young and in pretty good shape, so the platoon sergeant put me in front to set the pace. The older guys in the class would fuss at me: "Slow your younger ass down!" Cliff had trouble with this part of the training, so I slowed things down a bit to help him. After all, he had helped me. We just "scratched each other's backs."

The racial makeup was interesting. Out of the fifty candidates, seven were African-American. Remember this was for the whole state, too.

There was not one racial issue during the entire nine weeks. There was more separation when I got back to Tupelo than there was in Pearl.

As for blacks in leadership roles, we had one instructor who looked like me. He taught us defensive driving. I thought I knew how to drive, but I had the "brother lean," where I didn't sit up straight, just kinda leaned into the center of the car.

That was cool. But it wasn't defensive driving.

This instructor made you sit up straight and put that seat belt on. Of course, that was the safest, and I had to get away from the "brother lean." Cool doesn't make it in the force.

We went through high-speed chases and dodged the cones, getting through at high speeds without knocking the cone over. Most of us passed that fairly easily, but when you got into a "chase" and you had to be either the bad guy or the good guy, those cones could go whirling across the cement.

They also created mock scenes where you had to talk to witnesses (though once you got on the streets you had to develop your own style of interviewing). It simply differed with each person. Some were loud and authoritative; others were quiet and kind. Both could gather information.

Then we went into courtroom training. We had to learn exactly how a case goes from the scene to the courtroom. We had to practice testifying. We had to learn what matters and what doesn't and how to respond to the lawyers.

And, in the middle of that we learned what "WWW" meant way before it was the world wide web. Our WWW was Weekends Were Welcome!

We would pile in that old Buick and head north on a Friday afternoon. We took care of our parents or met with our girlfriends or just plain sat on the couch and watched TV. No homework. Then on Sundays, Cliff, Tyrone, and I would load up that old Buick and again drive south for the week.

Cliff didn't get stopped any more for speeding.

We blinked our eyes, and it was time for graduation.

Herman Hill – my law enforcement mentor – brought Momma, Melissa (my new girlfriend), and Herman's mother to see me graduate. I guess Momma must have been proud to know I wasn't following in Bennie and Larry's footsteps.

I can't put into words the pride I felt and the dedication I pledged as the officers pinned my badge on my uniform.

"On my honor, I will never betray my profession, my integrity, my character, or the public trust. I will always have the courage to hold myself and others accountable for our actions. I will always uphold the laws of my country, my community, and the agency I serve."

I have always hated when people take advantage of the kids and the elderly. Well, now I could stop it.

I was a cop.

Police academy graduation portrait, 1987

Chapter Six

Serving All the People

After graduation, I was eager to finally be a real policeman. They couldn't put me in the dispatch office this time. I was ready to be on the streets!

We gathered at the start of the shift on Monday. As the names were read aloud, it was clear there were invisible boundaries. Cliff joined an experienced white officer and went to the white neighborhoods. I was assigned to Marvin Brown, a black officer. We were to cover the black neighborhoods.

I immediately recognized there was a color line. Now, would I ever be able to cross it?

I'm sure their thinking was that we knew the black world and they knew the white world, but I felt it was a form of segregation. For the first time in my life, I felt the color of my skin had intervened. In any case, Marvin Brown had asked for me, so we set off in the squad car. I can't tell you how powerful I felt at that point.

Marvin deliberately chose me; he wanted to pass his hard-earned wisdom along to the next generation.

"I came here from the garbage department," he said. "They were doing that quota thing, and I got to be a policeman. I know the entire town because of my routes collecting the refuse from big homes and little homes. Apartments with swimming pools and low-income places that resembled urban ghettos. I know it all."

On the other hand, I knew how to read and write, and he didn't. So, we struck a deal: he would teach me what I needed to know to survive as a black cop in a Southern police department, and I would write the reports and read the orders. It worked.

My responsibility was just to write up what we did. For instance, one of his lessons for me was "Nobody ever got fired for *not* writing a ticket."

So, one time he said, "You see that guy run the red light?"

"No, sir, I didn't."

"Well, I saw him, and he did! So, write him a ticket."

But I soon learned we had to be careful who we wrote tickets to. If we went across Gloster Street to where the white folks live, we had better be very sure when we wrote a ticket that somebody doesn't call the chief and get it torn up before we even got back to the station. Marvin told me that I couldn't let someone go if somebody higher up thought I shouldn't.

He taught me to stay in the black area.

I will say this. Marvin Brown and his fellow black officers on the TPD knew about community policing long before it was a buzzword. They were doing it.

These guys *never* pulled their guns. In fact, the joke around the station was that their bullets had been in their guns so long they became rusty. Another joke was that one officer, George Warren (who we all called "Payday" because he was so happy on payday) only had one bullet in his gun, like Barny Fife in *Mayberry RFD*.

These men knew everyone in their district and could stop a fight with a sharp word.

"George! What you doin'? You get home to your wife and give her that paycheck!" And George would humbly slink away.

Marvin told me to write tickets when he said so, and not before. He and I took the 10 p.m. to 6 am shift. He would drive until about 3 in the morning, and then it was up to me to stay awake and drive from 3 until 6. He slept those three hours.

He also told me that first week, "You're going to be hit on by lots of women, but don't you do it. Lots of guys got in trouble and got fired for what goes on between a loose woman and a cop. You pay attention to Melissa!" Some guys got caught with a woman who got pregnant; others got into trouble when those women "had something" on them. But I'll tell you right now, that was one lesson I took from Marvin Brown, and I never had any problems. I'm glad he said all that.

Another important point he emphasized to me was, "Don't get in financial trouble!" He meant that I shouldn't get where I had to borrow money from anyone. That would mean they had it over me. They could come and ask for a "favor" that would be outside the law, and if I did it, I was indebted to that person.

In other words, I would be in deep trouble. He said the same thing about going to a finance company, too. He encouraged me to go to the bank if I needed money to buy a house, or a car.

"Don't go to any shady places. Only trouble lies ahead if you do."

Marvin came on the force in the years when they were trying to diversify racially. But he wasn't the only black on the force: as I said, there was also George Warren and Tyrone Ashby, whose father owned a store and was highly regarded in both the black and white communities. Marion Morrow was black, too.

I hated it when Marvin retired. He was my mentor; he was the man who gave me "the talk" that my daddy hadn't needed to give me but that is so necessary in today's world. I learned "how to be black" from him.

Marvin made it to sergeant in the ranks, and when Billy White became chief of police sometime in the '90s, Marvin asked him at a department meeting, "Will I ever get to another rank, or will I retire as a sergeant?" Billy told him, "Sure, Marvin, you'll advance – you're a good cop." But the rank advance never came, and he retired as a sergeant, just like he thought.

Now, I'm telling you that as I started to rise in the department, every time I made a new rank advancement, I got a call from Marvin. "Congratulations! Your troubles are about to start!" He was talking about the personal responses to a black man progressing.

"Is he jealous? Keep your eyes open. You won't have issues until you have a rank equal to or above white cops."

Mercifully, Marvin died before my troubles began.

There was a fraternity of policemen on the streets when I became a cop. When white guys needed black officers, they would call for help from them, and they would come.

For instance, I was riding in the car by myself when I got a call to come to the Waffle House. When I got there, I found a bunch of huge white guys in overalls with no shirts, slugging it out with each other. I was the first on site, so I said in my most authoritative voice, "Quit that fightin' or you're goin' to jail!"

One of the big guys turned around and said, "Who's gonna do it, you?" I was 5'9" and I weighed about 135 then.

I knew I might be in trouble.

Right then, Marvin and two white officers came in, and Marvin got to scuffling with one of the guys. The white officers arrested the others and got them into the car, but Marvin, the black officer, was having trouble getting his white guy in, so he started whacking the guy's legs, and the guy started yelling the "n" word and cussing. Marvin finally got him into the car with the others, and they headed out to the station.

When they got there, the white officer, a guy named Officer Sherfield, said to Marvin, "No…this one's mine!" He then proceeded to make sure that that white guy never called a black cop anything else but "sir" after that. Those guys just couldn't believe that a white cop would stand up for a black one.

They underestimated the fraternity of all policemen.

It happened in the reverse, too. About three months later, Marvin and I were working same shift, but in a different car, and were eating our dinner. We got a call from Cotton McCoy in the black area. Cotton told us to finish our dinner, but a few minutes later, he called again, asking for backup. So, we headed out.

He and Marvin entered the home of Moses Bush, a very large and very belligerent black man, where they found two white officers already wrestling with Moses, trying to get him under control. Now he was already drunk and mouthy, but he also had come home without the money he was supposed to bring to his wife. To say he was in trouble was an understatement.

Marvin walked in and said loudly, "Bush! Bush! What you doin'?"

Bush responded, "They came in and messed with me."

But when Marvin yelled at him, old Moses calmed down, and the police could get him under control to take him to the station. Working together is a two-way street.

I had a lot to learn, not the least of which was how to be a cop on a motorcycle.

"Brakes are here. Here's the gas, too. Just get on and ride."

That was the training I got in Cycle Riding 101. Thus began my time on motor assignment.

Swinging my leg over the seat, I tried to look confident as I straddled that beast. I started the engine, and it roared. I slowly left the police parking lot and headed out onto the open road.

It wasn't a pretty sight. People pointed and laughed at me as I rode through intersections. I was a spectacle as I wobbled from side to side, trying not to fall over. It was kind of like learning to swim by jumping in the deepest part of the river! I will never forget the faces of those folks as they watched me learn to ride that Harley.

I think they may have put me there because another black guy wanted it, but he had what we called "an attitude," and they couldn't trust him on the cycles. It wasn't the right thing to do, but I still believe that's why I was the one riding and not him.

It wasn't my favorite time either. Thank heavens I was only on that detail for about three months. I was glad when the detail was over and I could return to the warmth and safety of the squad car.

However today, I have a large, red Harley in my garage. You can't beat a warm spring or fall day with the wind blowing in your face and being free as a bird on the bike. I came to love it.

One night in possibly the first month of my job, I was riding alone in the patrol car when Dispatch came across the radio.

"Possible suicide on Lumpkin Street." I was close, so even though it was a white neighborhood, I drove over.

When I got there, I found lots of folks milling around in the yard.

"What's goin' on?" I asked.

"Think the old man in there offed himself," they said.

I asked if one of them wanted to go on in.

"Hell no. You're the policeman. You're getting paid to do this stuff."

Well, he was right. I was a paid employee of the City of Tupelo, so I went in.

The door was ajar, so I had no problem getting inside. First thing I saw was brain matter on the walls. It was, indeed, an old man – 70 years old – whose wife had recently died, who was in ill health, and who simply did not have anything to live for.

He took no chances. When I got in there, the 44-Magnum shotgun was still held tightly between his legs, and the back half of his head was blown off. His glasses were split in half, right in the middle. One half was all the way into the dining room on the table; the other was over by the window. There was the top half of his head, with pieces of the skull caught in the curtain. Pieces of his hair were on the ceiling, too. From the nose down, everything was connected to his body. If he had had his head, he would have been ready to talk to you.

There was the stench of death in the room and blood and flesh all around. A man who had nothing to live for.

That sight has never left my mind. Yet as a policeman, you begin to separate that experience from home and your personal life. If you can't do that, you'll never make a good officer.

I had another incident that sticks in my mind.

It was at a hole-in-the-wall place at Green and Tolbert Street: The Red Carpet, where they served fish and folks just hung out, drank, and played music. Iretta Getties (I'll never forget her name or her face) and another woman were fighting, and Iretta was as wild as a cat on spiked catnip and just plain crazy. She would yell and scream and fight and hit and even attack the police.

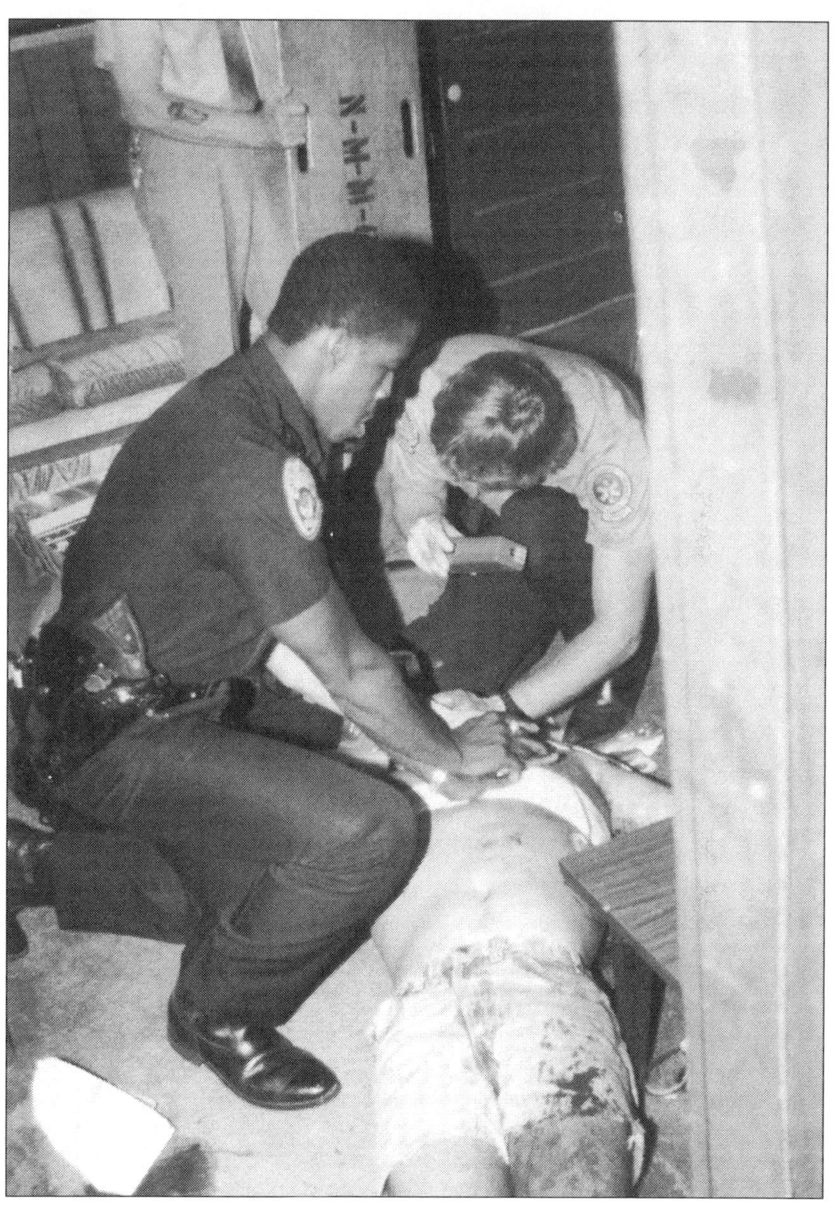

Working a gunshot call on the east side of Tupelo, 1988
Police Chief Ed Crider standing in background

They had always had a time getting her to the station. She was mouthy – just calling me everything all the way down to the station – fussing in loud and unladylike language, and by the time she stood there at booking, I had had enough!

I pulled back and slapped her good. She said, "So your little ass wants to fight?" and she came at me – all 135 pounds of me – and bit me on the chest. I still carry the scar.

The others got her off me, but I learned something that night. All the other cops knew she was mouthy, she was loud, but she wouldn't do anything except yell until she got tired, and then she would stop. Unless she was challenged. Then all hell broke loose.

And I, the 22-year old, 135-pound rookie, learned to let her ramble and rant. Let her yell at the top of her lungs, but don't respond.

Sometimes being the rookie on the force has its hard lessons. I see her downtown these days, and she gives me a sly smile – it reminds me in some way of our "encounter" that night. She won that battle, didn't she?

Right away I took measures to be sure nothing like that ever happened again! I went to the weight room at my apartment complex and started working out. My 135 pounds needed to be increased if I was to ever be able to deal with folks like Iretta.

Now there was a guy named Roy Crayon who was a bodybuilder – 6'4" and 400 lbs. He saw me struggling there and came over. He showed me things I needed to learn about and asked how much I weighed.

"135", I responded. He said he'd have me at 225 in three months. He said what I was doing wasn't going to add the pounds I needed.

I thought he was nuts. But he knew what was wrong and how to fix me.

"You need to build size," he said. So I showed him what I could do, and after I had bench pressed 135 pounds, eight sets of three each, I felt good.

That first day with Roy, I thought I was pretty good – I did what he'd asked me to do, and I was ready to clean up and head home.

"Where do you think you're going? You're not done yet," he said. And he put two 25-pound weights on the bars. "Now," he said, "Let's do some more." So, I did, but it wasn't easy. It was almost impossible.

"You're cocky enough, but you ain't big enough," he said.

And he was right. After all, Iretta had left a lifelong scar on my chest.

I was sweating so much that my shirt was dripping on the floor, and the droplets from my forehead rolled down my nose and off on the floor, too. And the smell! Even I couldn't stand that. Good thing they had showers there.

I stumbled upstairs to the apartment and collapsed. I hurt beyond description. I knew I had been pushed almost past my limit.

But you see, that's what Roy knew that I didn't. He was preparing me for survival on the streets, whether he recognized it or not. He made sure that when I thought I was done, when I had used up all my energy, I had to reach down – deep down – and find more to fight with. I had to be able to lift that extra weight in life – whether it be on the streets or when I was down, or whenever the Lord gave me more than I thought I could handle.

I had to keep thinking about that extra fifty pounds and that if I could lift it when I weighed 135 pounds, I could handle almost anything.

It took me really three or four years of constantly working out with him, but I got myself in fine shape. I bench pressed 225 pounds over twenty-six times. I read the NFL wannabees can only do 225 about fifteen times.

Roy wanted to be a policeman really bad, but he couldn't get through the academy because, with his size, running a mile and a half for as long as they required was just impossible. He was a cool guy, but he spent the rest of his time as a bodybuilder instead of a patrolman.

His "survival" practice hit home. I don't know if it was from his football experience, or if he thought I needed it as a cop or what, but when he taught me to reach down deep and give another 100 percent, I did. Consequently, I seldom had to use a gun. I dug deeply for the strength to do it without that kind of exchange if I could.

Another time, I happened to be sitting in the dispatch seat. A woman called in and said, "They're at it again."

"At what?" I asked.

"Those niggers down there are at it again – loud music, yelling, all that they do all the time, and I'm going to keep calling until you get those niggers shut up."

"We'll take care of it, ma'am." I responded. I never even thought of letting her know that I was African-American. "I'll send someone out right away."

She called back sometime later. "They got them niggers. They sure did. Thank you."

There are times as a law enforcement officer that you remember you are there for *all* the people, not just folks that look like you. That was one of my nights.

As I have said before, you learn your craft on the streets, and one of the interesting things I learned was about being "released to your own recognizance." By definition, that means you get to go home and not report to the police until some date and time in the future. Could be a court date or a hearing, or even a plea hearing.

Sure, the job of a policeman is to keep the bad guys off the streets, but sometimes you can do that better if you let them out first. Who gets let out? Well, not the ones we think are murderers or rapists or that kind of thing. People get released when they are known to the department: where they live, what they do for a living, all about their family situation. Sometimes we know that if we let them out until they set a trial date, we can even get more information about their crime or others we are pursuing. Letting folks go "to their own recognizance" is done often in law enforcement today. It can be the most advantageous procedure there is. There's more than one way to skin a cat.

Robert and Melissa's wedding, August 13, 1988
To Melissa's left, Rachel Kohlheim
To Robert's right, Rod Cobb

Chapter Seven

Getting Married

It was during these first few months on the job that I took Marvin Brown's advice: I got serious about Melissa.

I decided I wanted to marry Melissa for two reasons: first because I loved her, and second so I wouldn't have any trouble with the other kind of woman that was out there.

Rod and I had talked all through school about what kind of woman we wanted to marry: how they had to be good Christian women with good Christian values.

Melissa was a good example of that.

Besides, I had seen her mom in action. When her dad came home, he sat in his easy chair and didn't get up until it was time to take a bath and go to bed. His wife brought him his supper and he watched TV. She drew his bath, and he got up and bathed. He literally came home from work at the Super Sagless bed frame factory and sat in his chair and rested.

He took care of the man's side of the agreement. He paid the bills – she never worried about that at all. Her job was the home and the kids; his was the financial end of things and the outside part of the work – mowing the lawn and shoveling snow after the occasional storm. They had a clear division of labor. She had hers, and he had his.

Anyway, we were dating, and one day, Melissa told me, "You'll have to give me *three* rings, you know… a friendship ring, an engagement ring, and a wedding ring."

So I went and bought a friendship ring. It's probably turned green by now. It was not from a fancy jeweler, I can tell you that.

But we were committed to each other.

Well, one ring led to another, and between the friendship ring and the engagement ring, I had to ask her dad, Howard, for her hand in marriage.

We went outside her house one day and stood by the bed of his truck. I think my voice must have quivered as I said, "I want to ask you for permission to marry Melissa. I will take good care of her; I will protect her and keep her safe. I promise."

Brother Howard Monroe was known in the neighborhood and church as being super protective of his girls. You knew you could not mess with them, or he would come after you. He was the kind of daddy I wanted to be.

"You have my permission," he said, and reached out to shake my hand.

He and Mrs. Monroe took the next step: they went to the courthouse and signed the papers to give her permission to marry.

And before my 22nd birthday and her 20th birthday, we were wed.

The night before our wedding day, August 13, 1988, a few of my buddies went out to the store to grab some junk food on my last night as a bachelor. We didn't have a grand bachelor party – we were just headed to my apartment to enjoy each other's company and tell jokes that night.

As we were coming out of the store, a drunk white kid tried to start a fight with one of my friends. I stepped in and flashed my badge. "I am a cop, and if you don't shape up, I'll take you in!" I said.

But he was ready to fight with me! He said, "That badge ain't real, and you ain't a real cop, and I'm about to kick your ass!"

I couldn't believe it. Here this kid is so drunk he is challenging about seven black guys, and he wasn't going to back down!

Well, the lady inside the store had noticed the commotion and called 911. Within the blink of an eye, Marion Marrow had pulled his squad car up to the store, and he immediately took over.

Marrow was a short, stumpy fellow of about 320 pounds and 5'8" tall, but he thought of himself as quite a lady's man. He was always joking and calling me either "Ricket" or "Pipsqueak".

But that night, he knew that as I was a rookie, it would not look good on my record to see that I'd been involved in an altercation with a drunk white man. So he took over, took the guy to jail, and charged him.

He was taking care of me.

That got that settled without a battle, and we went on to celebrate.

Surprisingly, we were in bed by midnight. I wasn't going to be dragging myself out the next day – my *wedding* day! I was going to be ready.

And ready I was. At 4 p.m., all my buddies and I were dressed in white tuxedos and looking our best. When I got to the church, I was blown away. The families who attended there had outdone themselves. The place was so beautiful, I could hardly believe it.

And the best part was they did it all themselves. The decorations, the flowers, the cake, the food… It was unbelievable. But then, we were a community there. We all were part of the larger family, and since both Melissa and I had come from member families whose dads were both on the Board of Deacons, they went all out.

Before the wedding, Rod assured me that he was looking better than I was. He always said that, and he was probably right. His brother, Darryl, was close to me all the time that day, and he had heard that Melissa was crying. I thought it must be tears of happiness, but Darryl thought maybe she wanted out.

"Listen, Robert," he said. "Listen to me. If you don't want to go through with this, all you have to do is give me a secret signal – like *wink at me* – just a little private sign, and I'll take care of it. When the preacher says, 'Is there anyone here who objects to this union?' I'll be real loud, and say, 'I do!'"

'Course, I never winked, and he never had to yell, "I do!"

Before I knew it, I was standing in front of all those people and looking toward the door. I was scared, excited, and eager to get on with the ceremony.

The music started, and there was the most beautiful woman I had ever seen in my whole life, on the arm of her proud daddy. With slow and measured steps, they passed our family and friends and smiled at some of those standing to honor her. They made their way to my side, where he turned her arm over to me. "Her mother and I," he said when the preacher prompted, and with those words, gave his daughter to me.

The minister took over and repeated the oft-heard words of the wedding promises. Finally, it was our turn to make our vows.

"I do", I promised, and she quietly made her vows with the same phrase: "I do".

We celebrated in the church after the ceremony and later went back to my apartment. No honeymoon, no fancy trip, no fancy hotel room. We were very young, and, though I made a decent salary, we had no extra cash.

The next morning, she had Cocoa Puffs for breakfast, and I ate Corn Flakes.

And life went on.

Robert and Melissa in front of Robert's childhood home, 1987
In the background, Johnathan, Avita, Willie Dante, and Florine

Shooter's bond set at $1 million

By William Moore
Staff Writer

Bond was set at $1 million for a Tupelo man charged with shooting a 22-year-old convenience store clerk during an armed robbery.

Anthony Lenell Heavens, 19, of 522 Little Street, appeared before Lee County Justice Court Judge John Hoyt Sheffield Friday morning in connection with the Jan. 15 robbery and shooting at the Chevron One Stop at the intersection of Lumpkin and West Jackson.

During the arraignment, Tupelo Police Department detective Robert Hall told the judge that Heavens had fully cooperated with his department and had confessed.

Heavens said nothing during the arraignment except when asked direct questions by the judge.

"The victim was shot one time in the hip and the shooting took place after the robbery," Hall told the judge when asked particulars of the case. "He apparently felt she was running to the phone to call us (the police). He confessed that he already had the money at the time (of the shooting)."

Officials originally believed around $700 was stolen in the robbery but only just more than $100 was recovered from Heavens.

The name of the victim is not being released for fear of reprisal, said TPD chief of detectives Capt. Harold Chaffin.

Anthony Heavens, center, covers his face before judge John Hoyt Sheffield, left. Tupelo detective Robert Hall guards Heavens.

"The family asked that her actual condition not be released but what we're hearing is that she's going to be alright," said Chaffin.

According to Tupelo Police Chief Jerry Crocker, the incident began around 11 p.m. last Wednesday when a black male suspect wearing a stocking mask and brandishing a gun entered the convenience store.

Officers and detectives gathered information on a possible suspect and had Heavens in custody around 8:45 p.m. Jan. 16.

During the arrest at a North Green Street business and the subsequent search of Heavens' residence, officers found the mask, a .380-caliber semiautomatic pistol and ammunition.

Heavens has been charged with armed robbery and aggravated assault. The robbery charge carries up to life in prison. He could get 20 years on the assault charge.

At the time of his arrest, Heavens was on parole after spending time in the state penitentiary for possession of crack cocaine.

"We're taking steps toward revoking that," added Chaffin.

According to chief Crocker, Heavens was in possession of a stolen 1992 Chrysler Fifth Avenue that was used in the robbery at the time of arrest.

"But he didn't steal the car," said Crocker. "It was stolen from Coca-Cola and we think we know who stole it.

"We're looking at a further arrest and possibly charges of accessory to robbery"

Robert's first murder case as a detective

Chapter Eight

Becoming a Detective

I had two years or so on the streets, and it was just what I wanted: being close to the people. But our family had grown from just me to a wife and two kids. I loved my job as a cop, but the salary and schedule were not too compatible with family life. I'd always wanted to expand my horizons.

The chief called me in one day.

"We are enlarging the detective staff by two, and I'd like you to apply for the job."

I was competing against patrolmen with more education and who had more experience on the job. But the more I heard about it, the more I wanted it.

I decided to apply, and to my amazement, I was selected. I was a detective!

The other position they were hiring for was juvenile detective and who else was selected but my BFF, Cliff Hardy.

We both came off the streets at the same time. That was a bonus for us.

But, on the other hand, the troubles Marvin had warned me about might be beginning.

I was equal to the white officers now. But maybe this time it would be different and Marvin would be wrong.

A detective gets to come out of the uniform – the same one I was so proud to put on for the first time a few years ago. But those guys were the ones you called when there were problems; they were there to figure things out. It was a regular 8-5 shift, Monday through Friday, but you were on call all the time. In addition, you got your own car, and office!

What's not to like about that?

Cliff and I headed back down to the police academy at Pearl, where this time, we attended "Investigator's School".

There were lots of things to learn there, like how to work with fingerprints and put together the kit you take to a crime scene so you could retrieve pieces of evidence without compromising them.

Also, we learned how to help the victim think about the accused: putting hair styles or eye color on a picture that would eventually look like the person who committed the crime. Additionally, we were taught how to testify in court and make sure the evidence was as we said it was. The time went fast, and before we knew it, we were back in Tupelo.

We easily fell into the roles and activities of a detective. Go to a crime scene when called, gather evidence, work on possible leads and theories, and then hopefully be able to make an air-tight case against the perpetrators.

I liked being in an office and having regular hours. Being a detective was a good job.

But it did change our sleeping habits sometimes.

One night in June of 1991, the phone rang, piercing the dark of night.

I woke out of a deep sleep, rolled over, and picked it up off the nightstand before it could ring again. When I was promoted to detective and these calls started coming in after bedtime, I made myself a promise: that phone wouldn't ring twice. I would not let it wake Melissa up.

"Detective Hall here," I muttered.

Melissa, my patient wife, asked in a quiet, sleepy voice, "What is it, Robert?"

"Go back to sleep, honey. I'll take care of it."

I got up and stumbled into the kitchen to take the call.

"Let's start at the beginning, Officer. What exactly happened?"

"We've got a murder here at Crosstown. Guy survived long enough to get somebody to drive him to the hospital, but he died there."

"I'm coming."

Such is the life of a detective. You may not be walking the streets like the patrolmen, who are on a regular shift, working from 3 to 11 p.m. or 11 p.m. to 6 a.m. or 6 a.m. to 3 in the afternoon. No, you've got 8 to 5 hours like most everybody else in the real world.

Only thing is, you have to go when you are called. Even if it is at 3 in the morning.

I hung up, and within five minutes I had grabbed my clothes, kissed Melissa goodbye, and promised to see her before she went to school the next morning. She was a school teacher, and a darned good one.

She needed a good night's sleep.

I quickly got into the police department car that came with the job. I raced out our long driveway in Saltillo and onto the dark country road leading to the city of Tupelo, Mississippi.

As I sped along the way to the scene of the crime, I couldn't help but notice the beauty of the stars twinkling in the night sky. How could such a beautiful night also look down on the scene of a murder? How could the beauty of millions of stars in the sky be shining down on the body of a man with his basket of clean clothes who was lying in his own blood in the street? He had been shot in the very shadows of the laundry where, minutes before, he had folded his clothes.

The neon lights of Crosstown made the intersection look like daytime. I could see the yellow tape flapping in the breeze as the patrolmen were securing the area and keeping it from being contaminated. My friend Cliff and I were both there.

Here are the facts:

On June 26, 1991, a Tupelo man, Mr. Franks, was shot just three blocks from his home, near the laundromat at Crosstown. He was hit in the neck and yet was able to wave down a passing motorist to take him to the hospital, where he later died.

Earlier, Cliff had been in court with two African-American juveniles, Daryl Morgan and George Brown, who had been arrested for two burglaries. A single mother brought both of them to court, though they were not related. Cliff wanted the judge to hold them, but the court chose to release them based on their youth. We were both upset because the judge didn't follow our recommendations to put them in jail. We really thought they needed to be held.

After a couple of hours, checking out the scene and gathering the victim's information, we went home to sleep.

The next day, we got the description of the two males who were involved, and through confidential informants, we were able to track down the same two juveniles who had been released by the judge.

On June 28, we asked Daryl Morgan and George Brown if they knew anything they wanted to share about the murder. Both denied any knowledge of the killing. However, during our discussion, Morgan mentioned something about the murder that was not widely known: the killing had been committed with a "six-spinner" (a revolver).

It was enough for us to bring him in. He was no longer just a possible informant – he was a suspect.

An informant reported that George Brown was going around saying Daryl Morgan had done the killing, so we brought him in, too.

We interviewed them for eight to nine hours before Brown finally gave it up and flipped on Morgan.

Five years later in 1996, the case for the accused trigger man came to court. While there were witnesses in the case against him, Morgan's only defense witness simply placed him at that witness's home that evening. That person who was testifying for him had no idea where he went after 10:30, when he left the house.

Prosecution witnesses included another detective, Bart Aguirre, who testified that Morgan had, in fact, admitted to the murder. George Brown testified that Morgan had killed Franks when the robbery of Franks's truck went bad, and Frances Lusk said under oath that Morgan had stated to her at 5 p.m. that day that "he was going to kill him a person."

The jury came back with a guilty verdict for both boys: forty years for the accomplice (Brown), and life plus forty-five years for the killer (Morgan). He was lucky he didn't get the death penalty.

The assistant district attorney for that case was quite a man.

I remember one of his other cases. His closing argument that time was memorable. He dug around in his briefcase and pulled out a doughnut.

Yep, a doughnut…right out of the Krispy Kreme, I guessed.

He addressed the jury. "The defense has given you what's in the middle of this doughnut. That's right – he's given you *nothing*! Not a thing."

"Now, on the other hand, we have given you the solid meat of this case: we have told you the truth – these men are murderers. We have given you what surrounds the nothingness of this doughnut hole. We gave you something to chew on – we gave you the well-put together case – the delicious, sweet meat of the doughnut." And with that, he took the biggest bite out of that pastry. It was a bright spot of humor in an otherwise tragic case.

The Thomas-Morgan case eventually went to the Mississippi Supreme Court, where Justice Lee heard the appeals.

In the end, the appeals failed.

Three men had their futures seriously altered on that night. One man was dead, the accomplice served nearly two decades of his life before getting out on parole, and the killer is in prison for forty-five years.

When he comes out of prison, he will be 67 years old.

A couple of years ago, a guy came up to me and said, "You don't remember me, do you?" I had to admit I didn't.

George Brown continued, "You sent me to prison, but I have no beef with you. You treated me right. I just wanted you to know me. You said you would be in my corner if I told the truth. I could have been in there for life!"

That's one of the reasons I have loved protecting people. And this case kind of started both Cliff's and my careers as detectives.

We had other cases where our connections to the citizens paid off.

Both Cliff and I were respected on the streets because folks knew they could trust us.

We had a guy who would steal hubcaps to provide for his family. We knew him and his situation and tried to work with him.

We got a phone call one night with a guy saying, "Kentucky Fried Chicken's going to be robbed tonight. Two guys will hide behind the dumpster, and at closing time, the guy on the inside will leave the door unlocked." We recognized the voice as our hubcap guy.

The robbers would hold the gun on the inside worker, take the loot, and run, and then the manager would call the police. So, once the guys left the scene, we called that manager (the inside guy) and laid the case out to him. We emphasized what his role in it would cost him. He confessed.

The role of the snitch is critical. You could make some arguments about who's right and who's wrong, but we felt that the "good" guys in the streets trying to do right outweighed the bad guys who were stealing and carrying a gun. If we hadn't made a connection, we wouldn't be able to prevent the fast food robbery.

Even when we were arresting people, we always kept in mind that they were *people* – humans just like us who were afraid and made mistakes and had futures.

One day in 2024, I was interrupted while ordering my coffee at McAllister's.

"You don't remember me, do you?" said this pudgy black guy. I looked again more closely: he was short to medium height, brown hair, brown eyes, about 200 lbs. Maybe 45 years old. Looked pretty legitimate.

"No, I'm sorry, I don't," I responded.

"You arrested me once," he said. "And I haven't forgotten it."

"Refresh my memory, will you?" I asked pleasantly. I still didn't know who he was, and I wanted to be nice. The face was beginning to look a bit familiar, but I truly couldn't pull up the situation.

My mind ran through a rolodex of pictures – which case was this? And slowly, the years faded, and his current weight dropped, and his skinny young face came into focus.

Oh, yeah, I remember you now. He's the guy that held a doggone pistol aimed my head! A cocked .22 caliber six-shooter. And now, he was standing in front of me....

My memory carried me back.

Cliff and I were patrolling the city one night. There had been a rap concert at the Elks Club, and we got notice on the radio that there were 200 to 250 young folks standing around outside afterwards. A perfect formula for trouble.

We pulled up just as some kids started moving away from the center of the crowd, and here was this guy with a gun in his hand, pointing it around at folks.

Jumping out of the car, we ran toward him. Cliff had his .45 gun drawn, but he couldn't shoot because of possible collateral damage. I was intent on getting the gun from the guy before he hurt someone – including me! That gun was aimed straight at my head.

Outside that Elks Club for just an instant, my eyes locked in with his, and I saw his total panic and fear. He dropped the gun and started running.

I ran after him. He wasn't very fast, and I was in great shape, so I quickly caught up with him, got him on the ground, and cuffed him.

Both our hearts were beating like jackhammers.

We took him down to the station and booked him, and from there the procedure went as planned. He was indicted, pled guilty, and was sentenced to several years' incarceration, because brandishing a gun on a policeman is a felony. No jail time for them – you go to Parchman State Prison.

Twice in the ensuing years, Cliff and I went down to the state offices to hear a plea for him to get out early. Twice we said, "No. He is still a danger to society." Twice he was denied.

So, here we were in McAllister's, years later, neither of us with a gun, just chatting like two old friends.

"I remember you now," I said. "But let me ask you this: Were you treated fairly?" I ask that of all the ex-cons that come up to me.

"Yes, sir," he replied. "You were fair, and I was wrong. It was time for me to change my life."

"Did you?"

"Yes, sir, I did. I'm a supervisor in a factory, own a home, and have a wife and kids."

Now, I am proud to say that 100 percent of the replies to my question are positive.

"Yes, you were fair."

"Yes, I have changed my life."

Feels good to have a guy remember you for doing the appropriate thing and teaching them to go clean.

I guess Cliff and I were right that night.

A few years went by with Cliff and I as a good detective team. We had a record of solving cases that approached perfection. We liked what we were doing, and we were a good pair. In our time together, we did not have one complaint against our behavior when arresting suspects.

I'm very proud of that record.

The first formally trained TPD SWAT team, circa 1990
Robert on the left end

The SOG team, circa 1998
Left to right: John White, Robert, Trey Weaver

Chapter Nine

SWAT, SOG, and Community Policing

In 2019, a patrolman jumped out of a car, pulled his gun, and stopped a black man.

"Hands up!" he shouted at the supposed suspect.

Bishop Clarence Parks, who had led the Temple of Compassion and Deliverance in Tupelo, Mississippi, for 35 years, did as he was told.

That police officer didn't know that Bishop Parks had been a wonderful leader in the community for over three decades. He didn't know that he was a kind and faithful man who humbly served God and his congregation. All that officer saw was a black suspect — a threat.

Fast forward to 2022.

I went to the barber shop last week, where I've had my hair cut for years. After I got into the chair, I spoke to the barber, who is a friend of mine.

"Hey, Tom," I said. "Who's the officer that's working your area these days?"

Tom paused in his shearing. "I don't know," he responded.

"You remember Marvin Brown, don't you?"

"Sure, he used to come in here all the time. Like you… You come in here all the time, too."

But the current officer working Tom's area didn't take the time to come in and get to know the people on his beat. Therein lies a major problem.

When I was a kid, policemen were my neighbors or even, in some cases, relatives, and they often let me ride with them in the squad car. We were close to them, and they were close to us. Those black cops who partnered with me in the TPD when I first started were so acquainted with the community that they rarely, if ever, had to use their guns. They just called the offender by name and told them to quit. It worked because they knew everyone.

I can also look to my time as a dispatcher when I learned all about Tupelo, Mississippi – I knew the streets, the businesses, the schools, the hangouts, the churches, the homes… When I got out on patrol, I made friends with folks in those spots. Knowing people and having them know you is the key element in keeping the peace. They don't necessarily need to be afraid of you – they just need to know and trust you to do what you say you will do. Cliff and I always did that.

But even in rural areas like Lee County, Mississippi, the country was changing. Crime events were moving from something that happened in our neighborhoods where we knew who was causing the trouble to an anonymous perpetrator who would just as soon hurt or kill an innocent person. So policing had to change.

Some of the changes really started in the mid-1960s. Philadelphia and Los Angeles were the first two cities to create SWAT teams that looked more like military forces than the corner policeman.

Strategic Weapons and Tactics (SWAT) meant that this group of law enforcement folks was responding to special cases: threats to public safety which were not covered in normal law enforcement actions. In other words, we aren't talking about Bobby's Uncle Joe hitting his Aunt Mary or Grandpa Smith being drunk again.

No, SWAT meant lots of weapons and much more tactical training. It was a paramilitary unit whose discipline and skills went way beyond the normal patrolman on the streets.

And it became distanced from the citizens. Out of necessity, of course, but distanced anyway.

These teams were dealing with larger, more urban territories and sometimes with mentally affected perpetrators or terrorists who were armed and ready to die. Today, that military form of law enforcement is sometimes the only solution to a very difficult problem.

The War on Drugs, Civil Rights, and the 9/11 terrorist attack on the U.S. changed things dramatically. Local policing departments opted to create their own versions of the SWAT teams. And Tupelo Police Department was no different than thousands of other American towns.

The SWAT teams of the 21st century are different from what Tupelo created in the latter part of the 20th century. At that time, budgeting concerns meant that being part of the SWAT team was only a part of being a patrolman. You were issued a shotgun, a semi-automatic pistol, and a machine gun, but you got minimal training. You learned how to rappel from high buildings and even helicopters in order to take a dangerous criminal into custody.

I had to learn how to rappel out of helicopters well enough that I could teach others. Talk about a heavy responsibility! I had to make sure every guy on the team knew how to do it, not only to be an efficient policeman, but also to save his own life!

Those thoughts weighed heavy on me during that training.

The SWAT team was already in place when I came on board with the department in 1987. At that time, our work was clearly set out for us. However, the fault in the plan lay in the fact that SWAT was an as-needed job; the rest of the time, these guys were ordinary policemen. This meant that excess time was spent simply gathering the team together. It sometimes took as much as an hour or more. Thus, crime rates did not decline dramatically.

In fact, I imagine if you asked the average man or woman on the street in Tupelo if we had a SWAT team in place in the '90s, they wouldn't have had a clue.

By 1997, Chief Billy White and Mayor Jack Marshall decided to go a step further and create a unit called Special Operations Group (SOG) and

In rappelling training, circa 1990

Rappelling out of a helicopter was a requirement to become a certified Rappel Master

then to put community-orienting policing under that unit. The purpose was first to go after the bad guys, but while Cliff and I were responding to crimes and solving them, we weren't *preventing* them.

We were to take names and kick butts first. "We've got lawsuit money," the mayor and chief said. Our job was simple: just get this place cleaned up. Then using the Community Oriented Policing program, we were to begin to prevent crimes.

However, in our innocence, we screwed up. We were chasing the bad guys but not letting the people know what we were doing. So they began to see the guys in the black t-shirts (us) as harassing them!

We learned a valuable lesson. We had not dealt with relationships with the community before we went out there to patrol the city. It was almost backfiring. This was a two-way street. We had to let people in the community know what we were doing.

In 1994, the captain came to me and said, "I want to talk to you." I followed him into his office, where he told me that the department was to initiate a new "special" unit to work from 6 p.m. to 2 a.m. Tuesdays through Saturdays. It was to roam the entire city and take "hot" calls – disturbances, shootings, or situations when someone needed backup. It was a "floating" unit that had no specific geographic boundaries, but was responsible for the whole city. As a patrolman and former dispatcher, I knew all the neighborhoods and their residents. The citizens knew they could trust me, and they would tell me things. I would then pass that information on.

The mayor had asked for this action. Even with a SWAT team, he was getting complaints that crime was not being controlled.

Because the SWAT team was made up of ordinary patrolmen, all segments of the society were not being served equally. In addition, white people were being robbed on the streets. A political leader can only take so much flak, and then he or she has to take some action. The pressure becomes too great.

In the chief's office I could hear the mayor's voice, speaking with a great deal of authority. "Get these streets cleaned up! Clean up Haven Acres and Lawndale."

The chief agreed, and they put it to me. I was taken off of the detective unit and placed in charge of our new Special Operations Group.

"It'll take more money, cops, and weapons." I said.

The mayor responded at top volume: "I've got the money! I can provide legal defenses! Do what it takes to clean up the streets!"

"Yes, sir." And off I went, trying to create an effective unit of men who could clean up the city, protect the citizens, and make the mayor's life easier.

I learned from the movie *Lethal Weapon* about pulling together a group. I knew I had to have men who would give their all for each other, whether they liked the others or not. Men who would see the mission as I did: *fight to the death, if necessary, to protect the rights of the residents of Tupelo, no matter age, sex, class, color, or religion.* But for practical purposes, I had to have three black and three white members. Race mattered when you were dealing with a crisis. Sometimes, a black brother could relate in a way a white brother couldn't imagine, and vice versa. I needed both.

Remember Michael Jordan? He led the Chicago Bulls to six championships. Now, he knew how to build a team.

He had Scottie Pippen at his back. Pippen knew what Jordan was thinking and could mirror him in a heartbeat. He needed a "crazy" guy – that was Dennis Rodman. He could do anything on the court, but he respected Michael Jordan as the leader of the team. Steve Kerr was his skinny little white guy who could shoot the eyes out of that basket. He was so smart, and he knew the game. He caught Michael's vision for that game and could deliver.

So that's the way I built my SOG team. All the guys were ex-military, and I knew who would be my Scottie Pippen – Anthony Hill. He would have my back and the backs of the men on the team. He had the heart of the policeman, the heart of the player.

Now, the guy I chose to ride with me was Jim Palmer – he was white, but he could relate to blacks, whites, Hispanics, and anyone else! He could write reports, and he was a really smooth operator when he was on patrol. But if it got down to the nitty gritty, he was ready to fight if need be.

Another guy was Kenny Meaders. He had complaints on the streets every single day, I think. He was nicknamed "Robocop," because when things

The SOG team protecting BB King, circa 1998
Left to right: Jay Clark (later became a part of SOG), Trey Weaver, BB King, Robert, John White

went bad, Kenny was my Dennis Rodman. He went in, and he was mean. Nobody wanted to supervise him, and if he had just been on the streets, he would have been fired. But with our team, he was perfect.

Trey Weaver – he had started with the department when I did, and I put him with a cocky white guy, John White. They fought every night! But Trey could control John when push came to shove, and that's what it takes in those situations. One with a level head and one with a fiery brand. Together, they can make it work.

Anthony was with Kenny Meaders. Kenny respected Anthony and would listen to him. I trusted Anthony to be level-headed.

We also had a "dog" unit in SOG. One guy, one dog. They were partners, even though one was human and one was canine. I didn't have to build that relationship: it was already there! And they knew what to do in a narcotic situation. Chuck was my guy, and Mick was our dog.

We created a brotherhood. Not just a team, but a brotherhood.

We were men who would die for each other and our mission. We could socialize with each other, go into one another's houses, take another guy's wife to the doctor, pick the kids up from school. I mean, we would do anything for each other.

There was no black or white…we were all family.

One time, Chief Ron Smith was in charge, and he was supposed to make changes, because the streets were still pretty rough. Smith told me, "That house over there on Park Street… I get calls every day about that house. Something has to be done.

"I need you to do something. Shut. It. Down! There needs to be an article in the newspaper, and I want a report that I can take in front of the community."

We did it. We got the lease revoked, even though we never knew the names of the people who were involved. That house was empty. End of report.

SWAT and SOG coexisted. And between the two of them, complaints were answered, gangs disappeared or were incarcerated, and Tupelo did not become a mini-Memphis.

Today, the two units are relatively unknown, and our current Chief Quaka is working to get them reorganized. There was a time when SOG, driving our $50,000 squad cars with the weapons in the back, were seen as the *real* police in Tupelo, and that met with opposition on the force. So, when Chief Billy White left, the interim chief pulled SOG off the streets.

The reasons for that would be up for discussion, but suffice it to say that the citizens want SOG back, and Chief Quaka is working to integrate the original mission. People were safer then, and they want that same security today.

What I think it comes down to is this: community policing is using the relationships between law enforcement and citizens *before* we get into crimes and criminals.

Community Oriented Policing is the name given to what we were doing decades ago, where we walked the streets and knew the people. We called each other by name and knew everyone's kids and grandparents. We knew who was sick, we knew who had mental problems, we knew which husband would beat his wife unless we stopped him, and we knew who was out of a job and needed food. And sometimes we looked the other way when that guy stole a loaf of bread, or we went in later and paid for it ourselves.

Community policing is about building strong relationships between folks in town and cops. It means that both sides must be transparent and informative. It means trust must exist between the two. Do what you say you will do, never tell lies, follow through with your promises.

Build trust.

That's community policing.

What we were to do was to be responsive to complaints that the department had treated anyone unfairly. And there were plenty of complaints! Those came from the community.

The complaints centered on things like pulling guns, wrestling with suspects, anything that would happen when policemen would encounter suspects and treat them unfairly.

And what we had been asked to do in SOG was clean up the city, particularly in troubled areas such as Haven Acres, a real hot spot for trouble.

Now, let me tell you about Haven Acres. It was the Moore family farm in the days before 1945, and several siblings came into ownership of the land. By the 1960s, Tupelo leaders realized that the future was not in farming but in manufacturing, and they began to focus on enticing factories to the area. That made the cultivable area less valuable than before.

Willie Moore, a veteran, and his wife, Ophelene, decided they would take their land and sell it off for affordable housing for African Americans. It was a part of the American dream to own your own home, and Willie and Ophelene made it possible. The neighborhood grew into a sizable, identifiable area.

Life was good for the little community, and the adult offspring of residents moved up north for better paying jobs. St. Louis, Chicago, and Detroit were the destinations of our Haven Acres folks, where they found jobs with ease and began to earn another American dream: a good job and a good life. They would send money home to their parents, and in the summer, they would send their kids home to experience Mississippi and not be so vulnerable to the gangs that were beginning to show up in the cities of the Midwest.

What they didn't count on, though, was that the kids brought the gangs with them!

While the municipality was working to save their grandchildren, Lee County had taken little notice of the place and gave few services. Tupelo couldn't provide services outside the city limits. So the little village began to slowly decline like a vine needing water.

Soon, between the deteriorating services and the young outsiders trying to take over the place, Haven Acres was no longer a safe place to be.

When the chief began the Special Operations Group, roughly in the mid-1990's, the entire area could be called a gangbanging, crime-ridden place, with robberies, guys beating up their girlfriends, drag racing, drug dealing, murders, and other felonies going on. Some of the elderly citizens took to leaving their doors unlocked so that even if they were robbed, they wouldn't have to buy a new door, too! Others tried to sell their homes to get some money and get away from the crime. But nobody else wanted to buy property in that area, so it was well on its way to becoming a slum. Local citizens often reported that the word on the street was that the cops didn't even want to come to Haven Acres.

It was that bad.

And these were the people who had bought the land from Willie Moore with the idea of having the American dream.

There was a church in North Tupelo that had an outreach program perfectly designed to help those folks in Haven Acres. Spring Hill Baptist Church created a program to try to raise the quality of life for those people to meet their middle-class dreams.

Another movement that impacted the hamlet was an idea from a white Bible teacher from New York. Though he lived in a fairly affluent part of town, he really respected the law-abiding citizens of the post-WWII community. He knew only a few people in Tupelo because he was new, but among his acquaintances were the mayor's parents, Mr. and Mrs. Glenn McCullough, Sr. When the teacher invited them to join him on a visit to Haven Acres, they excitedly went along. The results of that trip were positive: the McCulloughs offered $1,000 toward the building of a community center – a donation that was to be matched by the citizens.

Part of their attempt to help folks was to pressure the mayor about involving the city in these works. That's how the mayor got the city's commitment, the money, and the idea of emphasizing the efforts to clean up this crime-ridden area.

Now I knew Haven Acres. I had made a few arrests there and had heard a few bad guys complain that the cops were picking on them. Normally, a cop would respond to a call there in a worn-out squad car and cruise the neighborhood, but they would usually not get out of the car. After a few circles around the blocks, that cop would drive out of the neighborhood and leave them alone.

We in SOG knew it would be a challenge, but we believed we were up to it. In fact, we had learned an important lesson from earlier operations. We would be totally transparent and require the same from the citizens of Haven Acres.

The reputation of being trustworthy, plus being black, was why I was chosen. The experiences that I had on the streets had given me the reputation of "doing what I said I would do."

SOG strategized about getting the job done. This time we wouldn't make the same mistake. We would be sure the citizens knew what was going on.

Transparency – that's the key to trust.

Most folks know that the church is the most important institution in the black community, and if you want to get the word out about anything, start with a meeting at the church. So, our first community gathering was at the Morning Star church in Haven Acres.

We gathered in the church in Haven Acres one night for our first meeting with the citizens. There were about thirty-five to forty people sitting in the audience, quietly talking to each other. The six of us, the SOG men, were in the front of the room with our black t-shirts on.

The meeting began and I spoke up. "Our purpose is to tell you who we are, what we want to do, how we want to connect with you, and exactly what is going on in your community."

I went on. "If we are to be successful at all, we have to work together. And if your grandchild is causing trouble, you have to back us up when we take the boy or girl in. If we find out that someone is beating up on his girlfriend, if she has even a scratch on her head, we will come after him and confront him. No one will be excused."

And in an effort to make a point, I said in a stern voice, "You want to know how serious we are? We're going to give you our beeper numbers and phone numbers. If you can't trust some of the officers, you can trust us! Call us instead of 911 when you need help."

So, after meeting all of them, we went back to the station to see if they trusted us enough to call. If they were pushed far enough to even turn in their own kin.

It wasn't long before we got the first deliberate call.

One of the folks who had attended the meeting called and said, "I'm down here in Haven Acres. You told me to call you – not 911, right? I'm talkin' to Robert Hall, right? Only Robert Hall… He's the guy that was at the church meeting? Right?"

"Absolutely. I'm right here," I responded.

He went on to be more specific about what was going on there. "These people are ganging up on the corner – gangbangers."

Now, I knew that these were the kids had the RAN group – "Real Acres Niggers" group – and they were part of the Vice Lords of California. They formed their own group with their own colors: red and white. The gang from further north in Tupelo wore blue and black and were called Black Gangsters – gangs who weren't afraid to fight. They had to rob or shoot someone to be a part of the gang. We ultimately had to deal with them.

Hard.

That call was Customer #1. Somebody trusted us.

It was sometime after that when Ms. Teena King called the police department. She saw a drug deal going down in front of her house, and she wanted to talk to me.

The TPD operator was polite, but said, "Officer Hall is very busy. May I take a message?"

"No! I'm not talking to anyone at all except Mr. Hall."

"But Ms. King, I told you he is a very busy man," the operator replied.

Now, Ms. King had made calls before and knew full well that a message didn't cut it. She wouldn't hear back. "I will just keep calling back until you put me through," she said loudly.

"Hello, Ms. King. How can I help you?" I asked when the operator reluctantly put her through.

"Now, Officer Hall, you came out and said you and your men would come out here if we called. I trust you to do that. There's a drug deal going down right in front of my house. Are you comin' out or not?"

"Now, Ms. King. Just tell me what is happening?" I asked patiently.

Her frustration showed in the volume of her voice. She fairly shouted into the phone, "I told you! There's a drug deal goin' on outside my house, and if you don't come down here and do something, I'm going outside in my robe and slippers and make a citizen's arrest!"

"Now Ms. King, don't go doin' that – you could get hurt, 'cause these folks can be dangerous. I will be there as soon as I can get in the patrol car and drive there, but you stay in your house."

"I don't care, you hear? I'm so tired of this nonsense goin' on and nobody doin' anything."

I ran out of the office, got in the squad car, and headed for Haven Acres. When I got there, the guys were still trying to do a deal by Ms. King's house.

I got out of my squad car and headed toward them, yelling as I walked. "Get out of here and don't come back for your deals, that clear? The next time, you're going to be in jail for sure." They attempted to continue, but when I repeated in an even louder voice, moving my hand on my sidearm, they began to disperse.

Ms. King was happy, and I hoped that they'd get the message.

We began doing "community policing," where a cop riding in the squad car would stop and get out and engage the citizens in conversations. The policeman would talk to the teenagers and get their attention and begin to earn their trust.

Before long, the streets got quieter and safer, and Haven Acres began to make progress toward their middle-class dream of a civic community.

By the mid- to late-'90s, the Haven Acres community was being acknowledged as a model for clearing out the ghetto and becoming a viable middle-class black village. In fact, we accompanied Dr. Vaughn Grisham as he spoke in Howard County, Texas, and Huntington, West Virginia, about their successes. At the meetings in West Virginia, the police officers attending sat with their bulging, muscular, white arms crossed over their broad chests (these guys were gym regulars and I knew it!) while I spoke. Their body language shouted that they didn't see that happening in their town. We were convinced that our message had not been heard. But about three weeks later, a member of the police force called to report that they were engaging in community policing there with success.

The chief from Huntington began. "Two of our cops got out of their car a week or so ago and got into a pickup game of basketball with some kids over at the projects. Before you knew it, the mommas came out.

"'Hey,' the cautious mommas said. 'Are the kids doing something wrong?'

"'No, ma'am. We just thought we'd play a bit of basketball with them.' Our officers replied in a very polite voice.

"Before you knew it, the kids, the cops, and the mommas were just getting to know each other. Everyone began to trust each other," the chief continued.

We were so proud of those guys who took a chance on our message and made it work.

Community policing at its best.

And there was clear documentation in Haven Acres that crime reports declined. The *Daily Journal* wrote extensively of the decline of crime in 1999 over 1998, including a nearly 50 percent decrease in property robberies.

Their dream of getting a community center for the Boys and Girls Club had been met by a promise from Phil Sullivan, the city's financial officer. If the citizens of Haven Acres could raise $25,000, the city would match it. By this time, the town was inside the city limits of Tupelo, and the city could work with them.

Well, they got to work. They had spaghetti dinners, car washes, and bake sales nearly every week. They were determined to raise that $25,000. And they did.

They went to Mr. Sullivan and reported their fundraising. He went to the city council and reported back to the Haven Acres representatives. Funds were low, they were told, but if they could raise $50,000, the city would double their contribution and give them $50,000 to build their center.

They went back to work. More spaghetti dinners, more bake sales, and the cleanest cars in town, thanks to all those car washes. Off they went again with their monies in their hand.

Mr. Sullivan reported it to the city, and the city again denied the ability to raise $50,000 for Haven Acres. But, for sure, if they raised $100,000, the city would come through with the money to help build their center for them.

Well, it shouldn't surprise you to know that those Haven Acres folks went back disgusted that the city would go back on their promises, but bound and determined they would win this battle and get their building.

People can eat a lot of spaghetti, and it's cheap. Soap for a car wash isn't very expensive, either, and lots of women can bake a multitude of cakes, and men and teenagers can eat them. I ate some of them myself.

For the third time, they headed to the city with their $100,000 in hand. Phil Sullivan reported to the council that he just could not deny these people their promise again.

Haven Acres got their community center, and it became a Boys and Girls Club.

In fact, when Dr. and Mrs. Grisham took a group from the community to speak at Howard Community College in Big Spring, Texas, Ms. Moore, one of the original founders of Haven Acres, got up to tell the neighborhood's story.

In her quiet Mississippi accent, she spun the tale of their successes. She told of having to name family members when crimes were committed and they were charged. She talked of the community coming together and raising the funds for the Boys and Girls Club. She didn't use fine English. She wasn't dressed in fashionable clothes with a matching hat and gloves and shoes. No, Ms. Moore stood there in her bedroom slippers and told the story as simply as she could, and when folks could see ordinary black people taking control of saving their community, they listened. They began to believe they could do it, too. They believed.

People gathering for a common goal – people trusting the police officers, and the officers trusting the people – partnerships based on professional friendships.

That's Community-Oriented Policing.

But some of those common elements of a partnership are missing in modern law enforcement. In an earlier time, policemen were walking a beat, and they knew everyone on the blocks they covered, from teenagers to senior citizens. They were friends whose task was to protect us. In the '40s and '50s, children learned in school that the policeman was their friend, someone you could always count on to take care of you.

With the advent of common use of the automobile and computers, things changed. Where formerly cops rode bikes or walked, now they became isolated in a car from those folks on the block. Distances between people grew wider and wider. Television kept people in their homes instead of on their porches, chatting with friends who walked by. With the Civil Rights era, violence in the streets between the races became more difficult to deal with, and policing returned to the militaristic model. Hierarchical and power-driven. Community policing had attempted to use the old model of knowing your neighbor. It was out of date.

Sometimes you could use community policing because you knew the guy and you could "talk him down". Sometimes he was armed, maybe drugged up, and there was no, "I'm Officer Hall. Would you please turn around so I can put these cuffs on you?" Sometimes they didn't understand you until they were face down, eating concrete.

But they always knew Cliff and I would never mistreat them. They would only get the amount of force they had pulled on us.

Looking at recent times, take the case of George Floyd in Minneapolis. The cop who had his knee on Floyd's neck was from the old, militaristic "scare the crap out of them" school. He believed fear was the only deterrent to crime and wanted to instill in those men that were on duty with him that you can only deal with these guys through dread and power.

Cliff and I would not have done that. There are other ways to achieve the desired outcome.

It all comes down to respect. Respect and trust. And that can't be instilled with fear.

All the time we were reducing the crime rate and making a difference in Tupelo with all the citizens, there was something missing. Both Cliff and I felt there was something wrong.

Increasingly, there was evidence that people were not being treated equally or honestly. For instance, there were complaints that when a suspect was apprehended, he was beaten and wounded, yet there was no response when interested parties would call the department and leave a message. They got no call back. In fact, there was no record in the department of any such event at all, yet photos existed to prove the individual was beaten up.

In addition, there was an absence of reports when folks had been apprehended. Clearly, the rules were not being followed the same way across the board.

But nothing was being done to change it.

At the FBI National Academy, 2001

Chapter Ten

My Watershed

Watershed: 1. An event or a period that is important because it represents a big change in how people do or think about something.

2. An area of high ground from which water flows down to a river.

Well, 2000 was a watershed time for me.

In the fall of 2000, Chief Ron Smith called me into his office.

"Robert," he said, "You're creating quite a record for yourself here. You've been an outstanding patrolman, have moved up to detective status, have led SOG, and are doing quite well there. Your accomplishments are outstanding. You've been promoted, and now you're a major in the department."

"Thank you, sir," I said, not knowing where this was going.

"I want to recommend you for a program at the FBI National Academy. I have spoken to the mayor, and he agrees. What do you think?"

My head was spinning. *I am a poor little ole black kid from rural Mississippi, and they want me to go to the Federal Bureau of Investigation? The key institution for law enforcement in our United States? The best in the world?* I knew my face must have revealed my awe at even mentioning my name in the same sentence as the FBI.

I had heard of the National Academy before, and I knew there were candidates from Tupelo that had gone there, but the officers chosen were always white men. I would be the first black man from our area to be selected for this program. I was stunned they asked me.

Chief Smith continued, "You'll spend ten weeks across from DC in Quantico, Virginia. You'll be training with the top policemen in the entire country. What do you think?" he asked again.

I knew the first thing I had to consider was Melissa. We had two young sons, and she was pregnant and due in August. I couldn't abandon her totally – not even for the FBI.

"Sir, I am honored, and I would love to be able to do that. However, I would have to come home a couple of times, because Melissa is pregnant, and I need to be with her and the boys. Could that be worked out?"

"Absolutely," he responded. The deal was done.

Now the FBI National Academy is a special ten-week program offered four times a year, and it's aimed at law enforcement leaders – not all practicing patrol officers. It includes people who are on the streets, in administration, in local police or sheriff's offices, and in military law enforcement. It is totally different from the FBI Academy, which trains folks to become FBI agents.

The National Academy focuses on people who are already employed in the field of law enforcement and is intended to professionalize that career beyond the initial state police academies. Candidates must be at least 25 years old and have been employed full time in a "duly-constituted" law enforcement agency at the local, county, or state level for at least five years. Education-wise, the nominee must have at least a GED and sixty hours of college coursework. They should preferably have a degree, but it's not required. Besides that, you have to be in great physical condition, and thanks to Iretta's attack and Roy Crayton's insistence on my muscle building program, I was in top-notch shape. My record showed "excellent character," and I did "enjoy a reputation for professional integrity." Lastly, I had to promise to stay in law enforcement for at least three years after completion of the end program. No big deal there.

Melissa, pregnant with Marissa, and Robert Terrell (left) and Brandon (center), 2001

I was almost shaking when I got in the car to drive home that day. It had felt like a really long day at work, and yet the ride home was over in a minute – or so it seemed.

I was so excited as I pulled into the garage that evening. I opened the door into the kitchen and said "Melissa, guess what! They want me to go to Quantico, VA and train at the FBI!" I knew what her response would be.

She is a queen of a person…just like her mom. The two of them are devoted to family and believe that whatever is good for Dad is good for the group.

"That's good, Robert. I'm behind you all the way."

The ensuing weeks were spent filling in applications and sending them to the FBI offices. Then they started their on-site work investigating me as a candidate.

That meant everything from talking to my best friends and some others to coming all the way to Tupelo to chat with neighbors, co-workers, and fellow students who had known me – anyone who could tell them what they wanted to know about me as a person, as a husband and father, as a citizen, and as a member of the Tupelo Police Department.

Eventually the word got out in the department, and while some folks were truly excited for me, I was told later that others quietly wondered why I was getting to go. They knew they could not probe the judgment of the chief, because he wouldn't put up with any questionable behavior. One of our men was going to represent the department in the FBI. He was very supportive of me.

But the whispering continued. My rank of major meant that I was already over many of the patrolmen, and I heard they felt that the "black man was becoming too powerful." No one said it to my face, but I found out later they said it to themselves and each other.

In addition, my rank meant that only the deputy chief was between me and the chief. And Chief Smith would not tolerate any crap. I had a dynamic unit on the street, and it was just impossibly tough for anyone to be openly racist in the department.

I ran patrolmen meetings at the beginning of the week, and 80 percent of the department was under my command at that time. The meeting was made up of all supervisors, roughly ten men. That meant there were two blacks – including Anthony Hill and me – and eight whites. In those meetings, I told them what we would be doing that week, and then I gave them their assignments.

I could feel an undercurrent in the room every time we met during those winter months. No one ever said anything, and yet it was uncomfortable; the body language was stiff and formal. It was like we were waiting for something, but I couldn't really tell what. I tried to be the same as I always had been, but I'm sure that my body was a bit more rigid than usual in response. I could sense it, but I truly did not know what was going on.

We just went about doing our jobs…protecting our citizens and assuming we were all on the same page.

Sometimes I wished I had just stayed a captain for my career, or maybe a lieutenant. But that wasn't the way God planned it for me.

It was good for the department to have a black man making professional advances. It was good for me; I had a family, and I wanted to provide the best I could for them. And it made me feel pretty good, too.

I was going to the FBI! I would be leaving my family for a long time, and would be far away.

The day I left, I finished packing my suitcase, left our bedroom, and walked out to the car. I put the case in the trunk and went back to Melissa's side. "I'll be able to come back three or four times before this is over, you know," I told her. I wasn't really abandoning her – it just sort of felt like it. "I love you." I said.

All four of us stood in the driveway. I spoke to my sons. "Y'all have to be the men in the family, you know. Momma is really going to need you while I am gone."

We hugged each other tightly, and there were tears in all our eyes. We'd never been away from each other for that length of time.

Then I turned to Melissa. Her usually laughing eyes looked sad.

I don't know if she could read the unease and worry on my face. Surely it was a reward for being a good cop for fifteen years, but I didn't really want to leave her and the children. I just plain hated leaving home – leaving Saltillo, Lee County, Tupelo, Mississippi, the South, where I knew lots of folks and the culture and the way my small world worked.

But I did think my daddy would be proud – I believed all those hours he spent picking up cans by the side of the road were worth it.

I kissed her goodbye, trying to memorize exactly what she looked like at that moment so I could remember her while we were apart.

That was the very point where my life began to flow in a different direction. I was headed to DC.

There on the seat beside me sat the directions I had printed out the night before: how to drive from Tupelo, Mississippi, to Quantico, Virginia. According to Google, it would take me about thirteen and a half hours to drive the nearly 900 miles. It was definitely a long journey, but in the cop car they gave me, I knew I could get to Fairfax, Virginia, that first day. Then, after a good night's sleep, I could easily cruise into Quantico before noon on Sunday. A forty-two-minute trip, so they said.

I turned the key, looked at my precious family, pulled the car out of the driveway, and headed east…right into the sun.

The department gave me a 1999 Ford Crown Victoria with the police package – black-tinted windows and a remote control that could even start the engine from a distance. I was in "high cotton," as they say in the South.

Now, remember we learned how to drive at high speeds at the academy, so I wasn't totally content to observe the speed limit. In fact, with my car labeled "Tupelo Police," I sort of had a license to drive fast.

And I did. While 70 miles per hour was the posted limit, 80 was my average, and there were times that I drove so fast, I'd have given myself a ticket!

The miles went by – some were slowed by traffic, especially around cities like Chattanooga, Knoxville, and Roanoke. Some went fast, like driving in those rural areas in Alabama and Tennessee and Virginia. Watching the terrain change as I went further into the mountains would have been fun to notice, but I wasn't paying attention. I just wanted to get there.

I did make it to Fairfax, Virginia, in really good time.

But, I must admit, during those long hours, if you'd asked me what was best about that trip, I'd have had to say "the time to think." I had a lot of that, and my mind wandered from being proud of myself to being scared to death…from wondering why in the world they chose me for these classes and understanding that they did it because they saw something in me that maybe I didn't see in myself. Course work there would be at the 400 level, which is senior and graduate level at a university. I had to learn the law, and I had to learn to write at a more formal and legalistic level. I had to remember many, many details.

I prayed on the way, too. "Lord, please help me do this. Please, please help me do this."

I had a good dinner when I arrived at Fairfax and a restless night's sleep after a call home. Sunday morning, I awoke and knew I was on the last leg of this trip. Still those insecurities invaded my mind.

I pulled out of the parking lot in Fairfax and headed north to Quantico.

FBI National Academy attendees at the White House, 2001
Wayne Capp on the left end, Robert on the right end

Chapter Eleven

At Quantico

Quantico is a Marine base near Washington, D.C., and when you arrive, you are entering a place where only those who have been cleared by the government can go.

I pulled up to the gate, and a Marine, looking very, *very* militaristic, stepped out of the gatehouse to greet me.

"Good morning, sir," he said. "May I see your ID?"

I was scared. Could I do the work? Would I let those folks who recommended me down? Maybe I should've stayed back home in Tupelo and forgotten about getting better. Forgotten about learning more. Forgotten about being "professional."

I handed all the material over. He looked carefully at it, checking the picture against my black face. It didn't seem to bother him that I wasn't white.

"Carry on," he said, and I drove on in.

It was like a college campus. Grass, trees, and brick buildings. It was one of those days in March when you aren't sure if it is still winter, because you feel spring trying to burst through. Crocuses were peeping their heads through the brown winter grasses, and you could not yet see the buds on the tree branches. It was so peaceful.

Just like at the police academy in Pearl, Sunday was the organization day. First, we went to the commissary and got our clothing. There wasn't actually a uniform you had to wear every day, but each guy had the same slacks and shirts to choose from daily. We had a military belt that went with the slacks, but it was "uniform" in that you wore that at Quantico during the academy classes. But if you went out to dinner sometime, you could wear your "civies". We also had short- and long-sleeved shirts and long pants, plus our "running" outfits – sweats. We had to be in great physical shape remember?

It was interesting, because that beautiful campus also had a training field track, which was used for the regular FBI Academy. That's where training to become an FBI agent took place. The kids training there were young – newbies who looked fresh out of college – where my friends all seemed to have a bit of gray in their hair.

One glance across that field revealed small groups of men and women running. Each group seemed to be identified with their own colors. It was like a rainbow running around the place. Marines were dressed in their running uniforms, and in the days that followed, we, too, had our own colors. The folks in my group wore green, and the young guys had blue. It was a way to distinguish all the folks who were running across the grounds. We all had a flag, too, with the same colors as our shirts. Pretty soon, we were all chanting some verses that were pertinent to our experiences at the time. You would often see a mixture of Marines, FBI trainees, and our guys all running in groups to get or stay in shape. Fitness matters when you are in the military or the FBI.

I guess you could almost use that image as an example of what I found in our National Academy class: a bunch of folks who were so different from each other. Not only were we from different parts of the country, but we were also from different nations. The FBI itself trains international groups as well as our own, so it was a real mixture of the peoples of the earth, so to speak. Real diversity.

We continued to settle in. Not everyone's classes were the same; we could choose "elective" courses, just like in college, aimed at what we wanted to focus on. There were courses centered on law, behavioral sciences, forensic science, terrorist mindsets, communication, health and fitness, and leadership development. I chose to "major" in health and fitness and leadership development.

We found our rooms. They were just like the ones in college – a room with two twin beds, two desks and chairs, a phone, bookcases, and closets. A door led to the bathroom, which we shared with two guys on the other side.

My roommate came through the door to settle in. He was from Mexico. He and his department were from abject poverty, plain and simple. They didn't have anything. He came over with the one bag he had and could only call home occasionally. He didn't even have a bulletproof vest, so, one time when I went back to Mississippi, I brought an old one back for him. Even in the budding spring, he almost froze to death at night because he wasn't used to being cold. As graduation came near, I realized he didn't own a tie, so I lent him one of mine for his picture. In fact, if you look closely at the "yearbook" we have, you'll see both our pictures show us wearing the same tie. Kinda funny – a poor kid from Mississippi lending a tie to a poor kid from Mexico.

Which one of these new faces would I be likely to get close to in the next ten weeks? I looked around at the other guys. Some looked like officers who were used to being "on the street," and others looked a bit more professional – sort of administrative-like.

A short, cocky white guy with cowboy boots who said he was from Montana walked up. That was about as far from black Mississippi as you can get and still be in the US. His name was Wayne Capp.

He's a real cracker, I thought to myself. "Cracker" is a semi-derogatory term we blacks use for whites. *I sure won't get close to him.*

He was from the West. I was from the South. He was Catholic. I am Baptist. I was spiritual. Wayne was not. He was raised wealthy, owning land in western Montana with cattle, and went to the university. I was poor, raised in a four-room home most of my life and getting into the community college because my friend gave me that dream and helped me achieve it.

We were both raised in an agricultural world, but his was extensive and prosperous, where mine was minimal and poor, so you can't really say we shared that background.

But we both liked cowboy boots!

Even though Wayne and I were as different as chalk and cheese, his care and compassion for family spoke to me. By the end of the ten weeks, we were so close I asked him to be my daughter's godfather. He agreed.

So much for first impressions.

I was set for the next ten weeks. Almost nine hundred miles away from home, lonesome for my family, but ready for this new challenge sort of in the shadows of our nation's capitol dome.

I slept well that night.

It was a life-changing ten weeks. As Wayne said, "No one goes to the National Academy and comes out the same." For me, there was the diversity of folks...not only from around the country but from all over the world. I had met foreigners before, but I'd never spent nearly three months with them.

Like Wayne, I think that the experience reshapes you in ways you don't realize until you're away from it. He says it enhances the qualities a person has. So, if you are giving, caring, and skilled as a leader, it will enhance those qualities. Unfortunately, if you are a guy who thinks he knows it all, it will add to that, too.

But for the most part, the changes are good. Part of the advantage is that you are far away from the demands of home, job, town, church, and the myriad number of other things that distract all of us most of the time. There is time to think, to evolve in those thoughts, and to be successful in various settings.

There's nothing to distract you. You can concentrate just on the subjects at hand. If I think of the changes I underwent, I would say that I learned to be confident when talking in front of a group of people. I wanted to share what I learned with everyone when I got back to Tupelo. I was sure they would all embrace what I had learned, as I did when I was learning it.

I majored in two things: health and fitness, and leadership development. Wayne majored in community policing. I couldn't wait to start.

It was like college, though a good bit more challenging than Northeast Mississippi Community College. There were different students in each class, and then, classes were at different times. I might have a break between classes to go back to the room and study or maybe stop for a cup of coffee in mid-morning. I can't recall all the specific classes I had, but I do remember the challenges.

Public Relations was a tough one. We were taught just what we could and could not discuss, how to deal with some issues when reporters were pressing us, and how to say, "I don't know the answer to that, but I'll find out and get back to you."

We had classes where the teacher lectured, and others where we had to do role playing. Our colleagues would sometimes yell questions at us.

"Do you have any suspects in mind?" "How exactly did that crime happen?" "Did the husband do it?" These were examples of what they might ask. They would pretend to be photographers, flash their lights like they were snapping pictures, and shove multiple microphones in our faces. In short, they were being generally obnoxious. You don't want to look like a deer in the headlights in public, you know. You're supposed to be the guy with all the answers. In the end, however, it was an experience in reality, and every time I see a chief or sheriff at the microphone, I remember those days.

That was a crazy class.

Classes also dealt with theoretical readings – an instructor would pull a series of articles out from professional periodicals and ask the class to discuss the various opinions, perceptions, and realities and then ask us to write a paper on it. This was where the differences in our backgrounds showed up and where we all came together to help one another.

We were a bunch of guys away from home, so we juggled down into our various cliques to keep each other company in our loneliness and to help each other when we needed it.

I was in pretty good shape, so I certainly knew my way around the gym. Well, Wayne and his buddies asked for my help with the equipment, and as Wayne says, "At first it's instructions on the equipment, then it's conversations about sports or something else, and soon, it's 'Let's go get a beer,' then it's dinner, and before you know it, you are sharing lots of stories about your life – past and present – and hopes for the future." That's how we got to be so close that I asked him to be my soon-to-be born daughter's godfather.

We were all in it together. And that creates a camaraderie that has few equals.

We often went to D.C. for dinner. Anything to get off the base, because there was not a lot going on there after classes. While Quantico was a pretty place, it was still a bit like being in prison.

Somebody would suggest, "Let's go to D.C. for the day. I'd like to see the White House." And we'd pile into somebody's car, dressed in our "civvies," and head for the nation's capital to find some good BBQ and sightsee. We'd ride over the bridge and into the heart of the city, seeing the sights from the outside.

Sometimes we walked the streets of the city just getting the feel of the place. We saw normal neighborhoods with other people walking around, and then we also saw important spots like the White House. I never got to tour the place, but I did see it when we drove by.

No matter how many times we headed over for a dinner or just to get off the base, I never got over that "bust out your chest" proud feeling.

I am in the center of the most powerful nation of the world, the center of power in my country – in the world, really. Here was where laws were made. Here was where many of the immigrants of the world wanted to come. America!

Back to academics: My final paper was a lengthy one that focused on crowd control and community policing. I proposed that a town of 32,000 citizens initiate a mounted police group. While it would be effective in dealing with Saturday night wildness under a full moon, it could also be a community policing influence. The horse would become an ambassador for children, teachers, parents, and other people. Too often, I maintained, law enforcement officers are distanced from the folks they serve, and neither group shows trust for the other. With a lack of trust, often violence breaks out.

Feeding horses, petting their noses, and asking questions is a way to bridge the gaps between communities and cops. Large cities have discov-

Left to right: Tony, Robert, Wayne Capp

Wayne Capp, Marissa Hall, and Robert, 2024

ered the wisdom of this, but I argued that we needed to figure out ways for smaller cities and towns to facilitate those mounted officers, too.

The teacher must have liked it, too, because I got an A. On reflection, I think maturity, just living to an older age, has a way of improving your grades. You are interested in what you are learning, and you see the practical application of it all. I could not have written such a paper at 18.

There were projects, too. Wayne had an interesting one in his Community Policing class. Hell's Angels – the nationally known motorcycle gang – had had a gathering which had caused a lot of controversy. Both of us were concerned with the citizens vs. rowdy folks.

The ten weeks seemed long when I thought about Melissa and the boys, but every day seemed to fly by because I was so interested in what I was learning. And yet, late at night, I often found myself thinking about her and the boys and what I was missing.

Two weeks between each visit was long enough. I don't know how Wayne went the entire summer without going home. I have to credit the Tupelo Police Department and the City of Tupelo, though. As part of our agreement, they flew me home every two weeks to see my wife and boys. I can tell you I would get in that TPD car, drive to Reagan Airport, park my car in the employees parking lot, and board the flight for the two-and-a-half-hour journey back to Mississippi. It was those visits that made my time away tolerable. Wayne didn't get to go home at all.

The grass got greener on the lawns of Quantico, and the spring flowers came and went. Before we knew it, we were preparing for graduation. My ten weeks at the most prestigious law enforcement institution in the USA, and conceivably the world, was drawing to a close.

There was a regular graduation ceremony, as you would expect, but there was also another very special event.

I'm not sure that most folks understand the emphasis placed on physical fitness in law enforcement. It takes a toned-up body to be able to chase these criminals all around neighborhoods, to corral and cuff them, to be able to climb fences or rappel out of helicopters to get closer to the suspect and disarm them. So, the FBI made fitness an integral part of our program.

Then there were guys like me who really like staying fit (so I didn't get another scar on my chest). Wayne and my other friends whom I met in the gym all went for the award in fitness – an extra indication that we had done more than was required.

The academy required that each graduate be able to run over a mile when they enrolled, and some candidates found that challenging. But if you had a real passion for gaining strength and being fit, you could work on getting the "Yellow Brick" award.

Back in the '80s, the FBI initiated a challenging obstacle course that took the runner through 6.1 miles of creeks, hills, and woods. Candidates had to jump through simulated windows, scale up rock faces with ropes, crawl under barbed wire in muddy water, maneuver across a cargo net, and more.

In the beginning, the route was marked by painted yellow bricks – easily seen even when the weather was bad. In 1988, they began giving special notice at the end of the program to those who had completed the "Yellow Brick Road".

Guess what the award was? A painted yellow brick.

I've still got mine where I can see it. It was hard to earn, and I'm proud of it.

In 1987, when I graduated from the police academy, my mom, Melissa (then my new girlfriend), and Anthony and Harold Hall (cousins of mine) were there. This time several years later, Melissa was pregnant, and Mom couldn't make the trip. But there was a video so I could show her me getting my certificate. That just had to do.

And then, it was June 8, 2001. Graduation. I had successfully completed the FBI National Academy program. I was a member of class 205 and a recipient of the Yellow Brick. Me, a poor black kid from northeast Mississippi.

I did it.

The stage was filled with the White House band – that brassy group that plays our patriotic songs at so many events. Behind them was a stage full of flags that represented all the nations whose law enforcement leaders

Robert's official FBI National Academy portrait

had studied there. People who had gone to the same classes I did, who went home and were able to use what they had learned. And people who went home to protect and defend the values of their nations.

I can't imagine being prouder of anything I would accomplish in my entire career.

The director of the Federal Bureau of Investigation, Louis Freeh, sat on the stage with other important folks. He and I had shared a 1.5 mile run one time. Director Freeh was an impressive leader, and I had been able to meet him person-to-person.

We lined up as the ceremonies were about to begin. Four of us who were quite close promised we would never lose touch with each other. We would always call and email, always be close. Wayne from Montana, Jimmy from New York, Anthony from Florida, and me from Mississippi.

That's the kind of bond you get after ten weeks together 24/7 in Quantico. Not quite like the brotherhood of SOG, but close. One man chose to come out of the closet while with his friends at the academy. That's close.

The music started, and we began our procession to the stage.

As I walked slowly in step to the music, instead of staring straight ahead, something drew my eyes to the right, and lo and behold! Four familiar faces grinned up at me from the audience.

Anthony Hill, John Clark, and Alex Norwood – all SOG unit guys – had made the trip from Tupelo to Quantico to see me graduate. One more guy came along, too – James King. He wasn't a SOG member, but he sure did want to be. I couldn't believe my eyes. All four of my closest friends at the department had flown in to celebrate my graduation.

It was my turn to walk across that stage and get my diploma from Louis Freeh.

I was floating on air, almost lightheaded. I had done it. I had not let any of my buddies in Tupelo down – those who had faith enough in me to send me that far away from home to learn to be an even better cop and share what I had learned.

After the ceremonies, I gathered my stuff and took it to the hotel my friends were staying at. I was out of my room at Quantico, so we all had to pile into the same small room. Then we headed down for a celebratory dinner. And we had fun. Such joy! Such teasing. Such friendship. Our "brotherhood".

They were to fly out the next day fairly early, so we all hit the sack before midnight, in spite of our partying. We had given up the staying up all night stuff.

But at 2 am, I couldn't sleep, so I got up, dressed, and headed to the car. I couldn't wait to get home to my family. I felt like a greyhound chasing a bunny – I couldn't go fast enough.

I drove straight through – all 900 miles of it. All thirteen hours and ten minutes of it. The dark night slowly gave way to a pink dawn at my back. The ribbons of highway led west, and the sun moved faster than I could drive.

I saw the rolling landscape of my birthplace as I drove through the Appalachian foothills. I was in Northeast Mississippi, where fields were filled with rows full of young cotton plants and dairy cows were grazing in pasture lands.

I knew I was home.

I could see the raging rivers of the world, moving in different directions than they had been headed before they reached their watershed.

I couldn't wait to begin my new direction.

All black FBI National Academy graduates of Class 205 (a class of 400 people)

Chapter Twelve

Deputy Chief, Ethics, and Punishment

I was back in the department after an exciting ten weeks away. I had been off in the nation's capital learning about law enforcement from the best of the best, and I was ready to share all the good things I had heard.

The other officers had been coasting along, doing just as they had done before I left.

I was the one who had changed. My job as a detective was the same, but I saw it in a different light. I had learned so much in Quantico that I wanted to implement back home in Tupelo, but many of the officers were not ready to change.

A couple of years later, Mayor Larry Otis called me and another officer to his office. We didn't know what to expect as we walked through the door.

"You are the third and fourth persons to know what I am going to share with you. It is an extremely important secret at this point. The chief will be leaving us soon, and we will need a replacement.

"You are both majors, and you have stellar records. I'm going to need you to make some decisions pretty soon."

Beyond that little bit of news, he added that the deputy chief would be removed from his position, too! Wow! What was going on here?

"So," he continued, "I'm going to need a deputy chief, too. Now, I'll ask the two of you to go off and discuss which of you should be the chief and which should be the deputy chief."

The difference between the two jobs is that the chief is the administrator. The deputy chief still is involved in casework. I could still be on the streets when asked to be, and I liked that.

I also did a quick review of my life so far. I had been on the force since 1987, and I was 37 years old. I had moved up from dispatcher before I went to the academy, and then I had become a sergeant, captain, detective, major, and a graduate of the FBI National Academy.

I had risen relatively fast. The other major was older and had a real ambition to become a chief. I wasn't at that stage yet. I really thought I needed more time under my belt. I needed to have more experience and be a bit older. So, he and I sat down to discuss the matter.

In the years since, I've gone over and over that conversation in my memories. I remember he told me that day, "I won't be working here very long, so if you support me for chief now, when I get ready to retire, I'll support you for the job."

I thought we were going to be like Batman and Robin.

And that's the way it went. I wasn't unhappy with that arrangement. It seemed to fit.

In a few days, Mayor Otis called a meeting of the entire department – all 100 or so employees. We met in a big room, and no one had any idea what it was all about. Absolute silence wrapped around all of us. No one wanted to chat.

Everyone in that room was scared but didn't know what to be scared about.

Mayor Otis walked to the center of the room and began to tell the story. "The chief and deputy chief of the Tupelo Police Department are no longer on the force."

An audible gasp went up from the crowd.

"From today on this man (pointing to the other major) will act as interim chief, and Robert Hall will be interim deputy chief."

We were interims only for a short while before Mayor Otis made it a permanent position.

And that's how I became deputy chief of the Tupelo Police Department.

I wish I could say all was good after that.

Because of our deep belief that policing is about building relationships, Cliff and I had a good reputation on the streets, as did the Special Operations Group. Folks out there who needed help called me, not the chief.

To the uninformed, it looked as though I were running the show, instead of him. But he was in administration, and I was in the trenches.

So, Cliff was back on the detective beat, and I was a deputy chief. I reported to the chief only and was the immediate leader of 80 percent of the staff and officers of the Tupelo Police Department. I was in that "no black man's territory" where whites had to answer to me. As my buddy had told me when I started on the force, "Your troubles begin when you rise up to where you are giving orders to the white man."

I could feel a chill in the air, yet I didn't really feel "outside" – or "not one of the men" yet.

The other thing I felt, though, was enthusiasm for my career, my city, and my department. My ten weeks in the rarified air of the FBI had really excited me about being a cop. I just loved my job.

And I couldn't wait to put into practice some of the great ideas I had heard about at the National Academy. Ideas from all over the world. Ideas that worked, as well as some things I had learned that didn't work.

But as Cliff and I did our jobs, it was evident that integrity within the department was still an issue. Complaints were often lodged at the TPD, and I wanted to protect the city and serve the people, as I had vowed to do.

Cliff and I kept talking about it. Where were the required reports on events? Why did the patrolmen and women not report the details of their arrests? Something was wrong, and when, at various times, we asked about these procedures, we were given vague answers.

Clearly, no one in the department seemed to feel it was an issue as much as Cliff and I did. So, Cliff got busy and searched for people who dealt with ethics and policemen. He discovered the work of Neal Trautman, director of National Institute of Ethics. He had often talked to policemen about that subject in their departments.

We thought that might be a good idea, so we asked the chief for permission and support to attend one of his seminars. With the approval of the city, we had the wonderful experience of sitting in the audience of Mr. Trautman's classes. Both of us left the meetings with a clear passion about needing to bring him to Tupelo. If we could convince the department of the importance of this man's teachings, clearly we would be protecting the city, as well as the individual officers, from legal troubles.

So, we came home with a goal in mind: hire Trautman and expose every member of the Tupelo Police Department to his practices.

We did arrange for *every single person* in the department to take Trautman's sessions over a three-day period. I can't say that everyone was happy about taking their own time to attend a day-long meeting telling them "how to be a great cop".

Trautman's book, *How to Be a Great Cop*, begins with the description of what kind of person it takes to be a cop.

> "They must remain alert during hours of monotonous patrol, yet react quickly when need be… Learn their patrol area so well they can recognize what's out of the ordinary… They must have initiative to perform their functions when their supervisor is miles away, yet be part of a strike force team under the direct command of a superior.
>
> "They must have curiosity tempered with tact, be skilled in questioning a traumatized victim or a suspected perpetrator. They must be brave enough to face an armed criminal, yet tender enough to help a woman deliver a baby. *They must maintain a balanced perspective in the face of the worst side of human nature, yet be objective enough in dealing with special interest groups…* [They must be] adept at firing weapons accurately… [Have] strength in applying techniques to defend themselves while apprehending a suspect *with a minimum of force.*

> "Then, when it's all over, they must be able to explain what happened – in writing – to someone who wasn't there in such a way that there is no opportunity for misunderstanding and to document their actions so they can relate their reasons years later."

Trautman's book discusses the canon of police ethics with emphases on protection of the citizens and upholding the laws of our constitution, among other things. But chief among this code, to me, is the section on the proper means to gain the ends… That is, you cannot use illegal means to reach a legal end.

No excessive use of force. No breaking the law just to get a suspect. Even suspects have rights.

Trautman also argued that community relations are among the first and most important issues in the world of law enforcement.

Reaching back into my memories of those times, I reflect on the elements of the oath of law enforcement officers that we take when we complete our police training and are officially hired.

"On my honor, I will never betray my integrity, my character, or the public trust. I will always have the courage to hold myself and others accountable for our actions. I will always maintain the highest ethical standards and uphold the values of my community and the agency I serve."

Officers in the Tupelo Police Department were not maintaining the highest ethical standards.

First, one of our officers shot a man in the back. Because his family and friends and other citizens were upset about that situation, the chief told me to go defend his actions to the concerned citizens. So, I did. I had to support that man's actions by repeating his description to the community members who had challenged it: he shot the man because he was turning to return the fire.

It was only after a couple of years that the other policeman on the site reported to me that the officer had, indeed, shot the black suspect in the back and stood and watched him bleed out and die before he called for help.

In the other officer's case, two officers had apprehended a suspect, and they cuffed the young African-American man. Then, without provocation the canine officer turned the police dog on the suspect. Snarling, growling, and screaming filled the air with the sounds of terror. Blood flowed onto the grass as the dog tore at the young black man's body. He survived, but he had to spend several days in the hospital, and he will never father children.

The reports indicated that this attack was completely uncalled for. The officer accompanying the canine officer did later testify that the suspect had completely surrendered. The dog was released after the man was totally under control.

I had to go back to this man's mother and convince her that the officer would be punished.

This was the second offense of this nature from this particular officer. My first recommendation was termination, and Cliff agreed.

The abuse of that young man went far beyond his initial crime of stealing candy and running out of the store, but the chief would not allow the man to be fired. Instead, the officer was reprimanded.

Clearly, the city could be at liability for that policeman's behavior. I wanted an investigation by the state police, but the chief refused that.

It is only my impression, but I do believe that he knew there were integrity issues with the department and did not want the state police involved.

At any rate, our initial partnership – our Batman and Robin relationship created on our advancement – was not operating at that point in time. My hands were tied, and justice would not be served.

I had a copy of the statement the chief had dictated to me on that officer's punishment. He did not sign off on this particular document, though it was my impression he agreed to it, since he had written and spoken it. But because he didn't sign off on that document, it meant that I alone was responsible. He was not held liable by the officer in question.

I would be the single focus of retaliation.

In discussing the matter with the chief, I realized there were people who wanted that officer fired, but the chief and another group of others did not.

The solution the chief came up with was 1) take away the dog, 2) demote the officer, and 3) put him back on the streets.

I met the officer to discuss his case and his future. His supervisor accompanied him to the meeting, which was fine with me. Interestingly, the chief did not join this meeting, leaving me as the officer in charge. I would have hoped that he would "have my back," but I was the lone administrator in that room.

As we spoke of the penalties, the officer got angrier and angrier. I could see he was outraged that I would dare to question his actions. Finally, he shot up and put his hand on his weapon. His supervisor immediately stood up, put his hand on the officer's hand, and said, "Let's get out of here."

Truth be told, in my opinion, the officer should have been terminated right then and there. But it seemed he and the chief were close. They both knew this was a valid issue, but the chief would not allow termination.

Later, the TPD and the city paid off multiple lawsuits on this same officer for his transgressions. Eventually, he had to be terminated because he was written up for repeated incidents of racism and sexism in the department.

I didn't realize it at the time, but that was the beginning of the end of my law enforcement career.

And this had happened after we had the ethics sessions. In the aftermath of all this, a morning call came in as I was getting dressed for work.

"You need to get on down here. You won't believe it." The flat tone of one of my black officers' voices came across the phone. I hurriedly threw on my uniform and drove down to the station.

When I walked into the squad room, my eyes were drawn to the corner, where a stuffed black bear hung by a noose.

I immediately reported it to my superior, who, I assume, reported it to his superior. Where it went after that, I do not know. I only know I never saw or heard about an investigation of the event.

There was no longer just a feeling of "chill". It was a reality. Totally cold – frigid. I was black and above some whites.

That wasn't all there was. Did you ever see the movie *Blazing Saddles*? It is a 1974 black satirical comedy about an African-American railroad worker who became the sheriff of a town.

"Black Bart" was the name of the sheriff. Well, one of the patrolmen in the department started to call me that, and it stuck.

Black Bart.

I'd never had "Black" attached to my name in my life before.

It didn't feel good. Especially since the guy who called me that had an office full of Confederate memorabilia – including the battle flag and Robert E. Lee stuff.

This officer preferred a certain parking place in the lot between us and the water company. An African-American woman liked it too, and when she got there first, he would pull as close to the driver side as he could get without scratching her car, lock his car, and go in. When she would emerge at 5 p.m. to go home, she would have to climb in the passenger side and scoot across the seat to be able to leave. Now, she was a young woman wearing dresses, and the actions necessary to get to the opposite side meant she had to do a lot of extra movement – which caused her dresses to "relocate" the hem lines. What she probably didn't know was that the same guy who called me "Black Bart" was sitting upstairs watching through the windows as she had to gyrate to get into the driver's seat. He and the other men there used to just laugh and laugh at her discomfort.

Such behavior made me mad. That was not why I became a policeman.

At one point, I was told that the chief had called a detective in and said, "Tell Robert that he is the deputy and I am the chief. He needs to play his cards right, and his day will come."

There was another time when the chief called me in and out of the blue said, "Lee County isn't ready for a black sheriff."

Now, you have to be elected to be a sheriff. And that position is a powerful one – combining politics and police power. But I had no interest in being the sheriff. I was happy at the TPD! The implication was that I couldn't win that election.

You're right! I couldn't win because I wasn't running! But somehow there was a rumor around that I was.

Internally, there were officers that ranked below me who would not include me in any discussions. They would go directly to the chief, which was not following the chain of command, but I didn't make a fuss over it. One officer – the man with the Confederate flags in his office – simply refused to meet with me at all.

But it was clear that people – some in powerful positions – were looking at me differently than before. I guess you could say it had been there all the time, but I had just refused to see it. I was more interested in helping children and the elderly.

Still, there were complaints from citizens that procedures weren't always being followed when black men were arrested. There was abuse, and when concerned individuals – from parents to preachers – called in for information, their calls were not returned.

This was the law enforcement world I had returned to after the FBI Academy. What I couldn't know is that it would get worse.

Much worse.

Of course, with all of this going on, there were still folks needing to be protected out there. One day when the chief was out, a call came through the chain of command to me.

"Got a call of a domestic situation in a high-end neighborhood in Tupelo. Man inside a home. He is armed and has his son and daughter in there with him. The wife got out and called police. We've got SWAT out there, but you probably ought to come on out."

I got in the car and zoomed out to that very upper-class area, where white folks lived.

When I got there, the tapes were up. Curious citizens had been cleared from the area, and our SWAT team was ready for action. It didn't matter if it was late afternoon on a Friday, that the guys were at the end of their shift. They were still full of piss and vinegar and ready to go on in and get the guy. They are always ready to bust down the door with guns a-blazing. There's a certain adrenaline to that.

Now, I had to do some quick thinking.

Here's a pair of kids – and I've got kids just like them – with their dad, who is distraught and has a gun. Their mom is on the outside, and the place is surrounded by cops with guns, ready to storm the place.

And I'm in charge.

First thing I'm thinking is, *We need to get a negotiator.* I ordered the call back to headquarters: "I'm going to need a negotiator. Can you get one for me?"

"Yes, sir. There is a guy ready, and he's just out of negotiator school."

Now, I know we all have to learn on the job – but this situation had *kids* involved. I had to think this through.

I had had negotiator training at the FBI Academy. I knew the principles. But I was a black man in a white world out there. I had to be careful about endangering a man and two kids, plus a few of my guys on the SWAT team.

My mind was spinning. I needed time. Plus, the guys were probably hungry since it was the end of the shift.

I talked to the guys on the SWAT team. "Get Curly at the Pizza Hut to send out pizzas here. You all need something to eat, and so do the folks inside." Curly is a great guy at one of the Pizza Huts in Tupelo who often sent food over to the station just because he knew our men. He was one of the good guys.

"And we need it ASAP!" I added.

He got those pizzas to the guys on the perimeter in record time. And we put pieces of pizza on the porch for the kids, too. We called their dad on their house line and told him what we were doing.

"We've ordered pizza for us and are going to send some in for you and your kids. We'll put the box on the porch. We won't rush you, shoot you, or anything. You'll be safe getting it." We put the box on the porch, the door opened, and an arm came out and grabbed it.

And I got time to think.

By that time in my life, I had three kids – two boys and a younger girl. I kept putting myself in that dad's place. I would never let *anything* hurt my children. Nothing ever would hurt my kids if I could help it.

Especially my girl. I love them all, but you just don't hurt your daughter. Not your girl.

So, we got a "bag phone" – there were no cell phones then – that would connect us directly to the irrational father. We told him what we were doing: we would get the phone so we could talk privately and put it on the front porch by the door. He was to open the door and slowly pick up the phone. No shots would be fired – no threat to his safety or that of his children. And he could go back inside.

It worked. We called him, and I began instructing our novice negotiator about what I wanted him to say.

I told him, "I want you to do the talking. You need the experience, but I'm going to tell you what to say. Okay?

"Talk to him about his kids. Like, 'The kids must be hungry.' 'This must be hard on the kids.' 'How are the kids doing?' 'How old are your kids?' Continue to focus on the children. Remind him of the outcome if he were to surrender – the kids would be safe, and he could be alive to see them graduate, get married, even live to be a grandpa. Discuss the impact of the entire domestic situation on these young folks. If he releases them and comes out with his hands up, things can be worked out."

In other words, take the focus off his problem and him and put it where it belonged: on the children.

Two and a half hours later, the situation was cleared. The SWAT team went in and took him without a bullet being fired, without a person being killed or injured, and with me drawing a long sigh of relief. The family settled their differences, as I remember, with only civil court involved. He may have been guilty of a few misdemeanors, but nothing that would require years in jail.

I had managed to navigate that situation successfully, but I had a firestorm ahead that would turn out even worse.

The site of The Incident

Chapter Thirteen

The Incident

"I'm heading out, honey. I think I'd better cruise the city to see how things are going today."

"Okay. When do you think you'll be back?" Melissa hollered from the kitchen.

I walked in, kissed her on the cheek, and said, "Probably before 10. I'm just going to be rolling through the town. I'm sure there's not much goin' on tonight."

I walked out of the door.

It was May 28, 2006, a quiet holiday Sunday evening in Tupelo, Mississippi. The coming summer heat was lurking in the shadows like a black cat, waiting to pounce.

I sauntered out of our house and got into the squad car – a black and white Ford with all the bells and whistles gifted to an officer of my grade.

As I rolled down our gravel driveway and onto the rural highway, I thought about the town I had vowed to protect. I had taken an oath nearly twenty years before to protect Tupelo and its citizens from harm – both their lives and their property – and I was still committed to that oath.

So, that night I was doing exactly what I said I would do: rolling all over town, down the main streets, and just looking around.

There was not a lot of traffic that day as I meandered through the streets and saw the residential areas of the old part of the city. Folks were packing up their barbeque equipment and lawn chairs as sundown drenched the entire place with orange and red and purple colors. The first celebration of summer was ending.

Yes, officially summer was here now. We are as hot as the hinges of Hades during that time, and everywhere you looked you saw half naked kids jumping through hoses, riding their bikes, yelling at each other as they played tag, or swimming in outdoor pools. People were sitting on their porches, swinging and laughing with friends and family under rapidly turning fans. Sometimes someone would play a guitar and folks would either listen or sing. And you saw closed doors and heard air conditioner motors loudly humming as they pushed that cool air around the inside of the homes. We might complain about the heat, but we love living here: it's home.

Conversations on the car-to-car radio with other cops always kept me alert and in touch with other cruisers on duty.

"What are you doin' tomorrow?"

"Oh, taking the family swimming out at the lake. Kids love to be over there – either puttin' a line in the water and pulling out those fish or padding around the shoreline," replied one of my buddies.

"Well," I said, "I had the chance to go hear some gospel music tonight, but I thought since the chief is out of town, I'd better just drive around the area to take a reading of how quiet things are."

I continued driving across the railroad tracks, through the North Green Street neighborhood where a lot of African Americans live (and some places where they got into trouble). Heading south, I cruised through the black subdivision called Haven Acres. Again, I saw no trouble – just a few older people having a good time with family and friends.

I headed toward the skating rink on West Main Street, just past Walmart. Every Sunday night about 1,000 to 1,500 kids showed up there, and all us cops wanted them to be safe. Heaven knows they grow up fast enough these days without any extra trouble to thrust them into adulthood too early.

My private phone rang, but when I checked it, it was a number I didn't recognize. I put it back in my pocket and kept on driving. I was already getting eager to get back to the house.

It wasn't five minutes until my phone rang again. It was home, so I had to answer.

"Hey, Melissa. What's up?"

"Robert, it's Diane Denton from church. She's frantic. The police have arrested her son, Allan. I think you'd better return her call."

"Will do." I dialed the unfamiliar number that had just called.

"Robert! Allan called me from the Hardee's drive-in restaurant over on Main Street just a few minutes ago. He said he thought he hit something but wasn't sure. He pulled over, got out, but saw nothing."

"Wait a minute – who or where and how did he hit something?" I interjected.

She continued a bit more slowly. "He was coming back from a holiday cookout, and when he got on McCulloch, right where Glouster feeds in, he thought he felt something hit the car. He stopped, got out, and looked around, but didn't find anything, so he went on to Hardee's to get to a phone to call me. He said he didn't see a thing, Robert, not a thing!"

After Diane's call, I put it into high gear and headed to Hardee's. I didn't put the siren on; no real need to, because in the dusky sunset of this quiet Sunday, there wasn't much traffic, even as I ventured back to the center of town.

I deliberately took the route that went by where Allan said he felt the impact.

Deep shadows engulfed the area, and it was quiet as snow falling in winter.

Funny, I thought to myself. Normally an accident scene would be crawling with people, and in the encroaching darkness of night, there would be headlights circling around the area. The uniformed men and women would be bent over, looking for evidence, and the most important person – the specialist who recreates the components of the accident – would be measuring, examining, and looking over the grass, the brush, and the entire area, literally with a fine-toothed comb. The tiniest bit of evidence could be a key to unlocking the incident.

But there was not a soul there. No one.

I called the station. "You got a call to pick up some kid at Hardee's?"

"Sure do," the dispatcher replied.

"That's right," the supervisor added. They were both on the line.

"Who are the officers responding to the call?" I heard the dispatcher shuffle her papers before responding with two names.

Dammit! My heart sank with a thud.

It was two white men who were known around the department for their frequent mistreatment of African-Americans. "Excessive force" and "police brutality" were the terms used to describe the behavior in such cases. However, at this time, Michael Brown was still running around in Ferguson, Missouri, and George Floyd was nowhere in sight in Minneapolis, so the issue was not as public as it is today.

All I knew was they were trouble to young black men – guilty or innocent.

I turned the car toward the middle of town, and even on Main Street, traffic was as scarce as feathers on a fish. Only a few cars were parked as I headed east.

I didn't want to disturb the chief while he was on vacation, but I was more than a little uneasy about this situation. I felt I needed his input on this.

"Chief", I said, "I'm sorry to bother you on your holiday, but I'm in a situation here I'm not happy with." I proceeded to tell him all about it, from Allan getting out to check for anything, to the names of the two officers who were sent out to arrest him. I detailed how I feared for Allan's safety if they were allowed to bring him in, given their records. I reminded him that one officer was the man who had turned a police dog loose on a suspect who was already handcuffed and under control, maiming him for life.

The second policeman, who, incidentally, left the force two weeks after this incident, was the man who had shot a black suspect in the back and watched him bleed out before calling for help.

These were the two men assigned to take Allan to the jail.

Yes, I was afraid for any young black man under the control of these two men.

"What should I do?" I asked the chief.

"Robert, I have great faith in your decisions. Whatever you decide to do, I will back you. You can count on it."

"Okay, Chief."

Hardee's was closed by the time I got there. Only the security lights shone in circles on the pavement, and the signs were lit up, too. Except for a couple of cars, the parking lot was empty.

I pulled in, and before I could get out of the car, Allan's family ran over to me, all of them ranting and tripping over themselves to tell me what they had seen.

"Robert, they threw him up over the hood of the car. They handcuffed him, and he was doing everything they told him to do. But the worst thing was we heard one of them say, 'You hit a white kid on a bike, and your black ass ought to be dead!'"

The family told me they had quietly stood in obedience as the cops had dragged him from the hood of the car. One of them had put his hand on Allan's head, shoved him in the cop car, and driven off.

Picking up my phone, I called the station.

"Is Allan Denton there?"

"Yes," answered the dispatcher.

"Have you called the hospital to see what the boy's condition is?"

The supervisor, who was on the line, too, responded, "Yes. They indicated his injuries were such that he would be released after they took care of him."

"Has Allan been booked?"

"No," came the answer.

"Thank you, God." I knew what could happen when a black man was arrested. Nothing occurred on the way to the police station. No, it was too public.

But when the accused was forced to go to the "changing room" – that steel-lined, cold-as-ice room where suspects are required to strip down to their birthday suit – they must endure the cavity examinations and were subjected to a shower and then dressed in jail uniforms. Well, that was a dangerous place to be. No cameras, no other people, just the suspect and the arresting officers in a dark, dangerous dungeon.

That was often when the trouble happened. That was where some cops felt they had the right to physically punish the suspect. In their own minds, they assumed the arrested party was guilty.

Getting beat up, having foreign objects jammed into their bodies, being insulted and humiliated. Those things happened in a changing room.

That's what I didn't want to happen to Allan Denton.

I made my decision.

"OK then. Tell those officers to return him to Hardee's. I am here with the family, and I am going to release Allan Denton on his own recognizance."

"Yes, sir."

We didn't stand in that dark parking lot for very long before the squad cars turned in.

Allan got out and walked quickly toward his family. That family group stayed far away from me as I walked toward five white men in blue.

I was tense, yes, but I was also angry that they were known for abusing young black males. It wouldn't happen on my watch.

The five men were standing with their feet firmly planted and their arms folded across their chests. Their body language spoke volumes to me, but I believed they would respect me, my position, and my decision.

I drew in my breath. "I have discussed this case with the chief before I took this action, and I have his permission to do as I see fit.

"I am going to release Denton to his own recognizance for the moment. He will report to the department on Tuesday after the holiday for further action on this incident."

With that, one of the officers turned on a dime and stomped to his car. He threw open the door, got in, and squealed his wheels as he sped off. The other officers who I had warned the chief about followed suit.

The two remaining cops stuck around with me.

I was left with them, the family members, and Allan.

This 19-year old man stood in front of me like a whipped puppy as I read him the riot act. In no uncertain terms, I said, "Man, you are in deep trouble."

In a faint voice he said, "Yes, sir."

I then told him what he would have to do next week. I did not know exactly what the charges would be, but he would have to show up and face the music.

"Do you hear me?" I asked. "You must be at the police department Tuesday to see what happens next. This is no small incident."

I could tell by the look on his face that he realized the severity of the situation.

Here he was, accused of driving while drunk – though the officers had not observed him in the act of driving. He had refused to take a breathalyzer, so there was no evidence that he had been consuming alcohol.

But, after nearly twenty years on the force, if there is one thing I knew, it was what a drunkard looks and behaves like.

Count on that.

I know a drunk when I see one, and Allan was not drunk.

He would also be charged with leaving the scene of an accident. His mom told me he had gotten out of the car and looked around but found nothing and no one in the area.

Did he hit the kid? I don't know. Had he had a beer? I didn't know that either. What I did know is that even if someone had broken the law, they had rights under the Constitution.

And I wasn't convinced that Allan's rights would be respected. So, if I guaranteed that he went home with his parents that night and showed up at Tupelo Police Department later, I had met my duty for the case. I wasn't part of the arrest, nor was I part of the case at all. I had done my job.

The Dentons went home, and I rolled around a while more before heading home.

I knew there was anger in that icy encounter with those policemen, but I had no idea of the fury they felt.

I had gotten the situation in order, I had protected the citizens against a so-called "drunk driver," and I had protected the subject against potentially abusive officers. I had seen to it that the perpetrator would be in the police department the day after the holiday, and the case was closed as far as I was concerned.

After that, it would be up to the officers, Allan, and the courts to decide his innocence or guilt and his penalty.

I was out of the case altogether.

I went to work on Tuesday as usual, and for the next almost two weeks, all was normal.

Two weeks later, the shit hit the fan.

Chapter Fourteen

The Calm Before the Storm

As I look back now, after fifteen years, I still feel the anguish of the weeks that followed the Allan Denton incident. I felt like I was an economic version of George Floyd, the black man who later died when a racist cop kept his knee on Floyd's neck after he was under control. That was "excessive use of force."

Reflecting on the past, I believe those who were against me just wanted to take the life out of me by throwing me back into the poverty where I had been raised. They would take away my salary and dishonor my name to where I could never get a job in law enforcement again.

They would make sure I would stay in "my place."

It was two weeks after the Allan Denton incident.

My decision to send him home with his parents, based on the complaint record of abuses by the arresting officers, was valid, in my opinion. He and his parents promised to return him to the station the next working day. This practice called, "releasing to one's own recognizance" was used often in policing, but this time, it meant that *I*, Robert Earl Hall, was the one who would be punished for my professional judgment.

I had no idea how bad it would get.

In the two weeks following the incident, my friend and colleague Cliff began doing his job as internal affairs officer, investigating the Denton affair. He was obligated to talk to the families involved to be sure there was nothing wrong, that there had been appropriate behavior, and that all parties were satisfied with the situation. That's the job of the internal affairs officer.

He talked to the family of the boy on the bike, all of whom were okay with the situation, and to the family of the driver. Again, all of them were okay with the situation.

He was simply acting as a responsible officer of the law.

About that same time, Cliff and I remembered that we had been approved to attend a community policing conference in Washington, D.C. So, we asked the chief if that was still on.

"Sure," he said. "The money has been allocated. Really, this will blow over. You'll be back on the job soon. Just go to the conference."

You know that meant a lot of money to the city. They paid for our transportation, hotel, conference costs, and food. It meant probably a $3,000 to $5,000 expense. But Chief said to go on, so we did.

One exciting thing came out of the conference (besides the information I learned) was that I got to meet Peyton Manning. He was one of the speakers, and I decided I would just go up there and flat-out introduce myself to him. I went up and touched his shoulder as he was sitting. He stood up and looked me in the eye, and I remembered that was one of the things Mom always taught me: always look people in the eye. Then he shook my hand. Boy, I thought I had big hands, but his hands were huge!

On the first day of the conference, I went to the morning sessions and then went back to the room to call Melissa.

"You are all over the news," she said. "One of Tupelo's top cops is off the job." She read the headlines to me.

I think that's why they got us out of town. They could release the news and we – especially Cliff – would not be there to object.

The media were full of the story of a drunken driver who had hit a young boy on a bike and left the scene. And how I had let this guy go because he was black.

It was hard to continue to attend those meetings, but I did it anyway.

Cliff was so angry, and I was, too, but it is probably good we were away. The two of us had time to "cool off" a bit before we hit Tupelo.

Chapter Fifteen

The First Suspension

It was the second Monday after the Allan Denton incident. The first week had gone by as "normal" – I would go into the police department administration area and pass by the chief's office.

"Hey," I would say, and he would look up and say "Hey" back to me.

I would walk to my own office down the hall, sit down, and open the computer to see what we had on the schedule for that day. Later, the chief would amble down from his place, and we'd discuss the daily plans for the force. Sometimes there would not be much of a critical nature. Other times, there would be something we really had to act on.

The chief's job was mostly administrative, and mine was a combination, but I would often make the decisions for actions to be taken.

The second Monday after our conference and the newspaper stories about me, I passed the chief's office, said my usual "Hey," but he didn't respond. He didn't even look up.

That's funny, I thought.

I went on and got busy reading the materials that had come in overnight. The chief appeared at my door and, instead of sitting down, stood there and said, "Could you come down to my office, please?"

"Sure," I said. "I'll be there in just a minute."

He had seemed stiff, awkward, and ill at ease, but I figured he had something else on his mind. Maybe we needed to meet with some of the city officials. Maybe a citizen had made a complaint I would have to act on. I didn't know.

I had no idea.

A few minutes later, I stuck my head around his door, and he invited me in. He closed the door and sat down.

Now, police officers are taught to observe personal behavior patterns and perhaps determine the mindset of the individual being watched. Well, I had long ago identified the chief's personal patterns of action that revealed what was going on in his head.

So, picture this: he was a tall man, 6'3" or 6'4", and he had a rather protruding stomach. His gun and his body didn't fit in the chair at the same time, so he would have to take his gun out of his holster and put it in a drawer. His belt usually sat above his waist, and when he reclined in his desk chair, he would rock back and forth and put his hands over his gut.

And if he was stressed, he would wring his hands, one over the other, time and time again. It was a very telling action.

With his grim face and his wringing hands, I knew there was something wrong. Must have to do with one of the hundreds of cases that we all were working on.

The chief drew in a long breath and began speaking in an unfamiliar, tense tone of voice. "I just wanted to let you know that we have started an investigation into your actions on that Allan Denton case. It's no big deal. A lot of the officers are complaining."

At this point, I was thinking, *Yeah, two* white *officers.* Was it that the driver's family was black, I was black, and the boy on the bike was white? Were they angry at the way I had talked to them that night? I still had no idea what I had done wrong.

He went on. "I'll place you on suspension with pay while this investigation is going on." He also forbade me to see any of the records of this encounter – the officers' reports, the hospital records – any official information about the entire incident.

I was stunned.

"Chief, you know what went on that night, because I called you and we talked about it. You gave me your support on my action because you knew the record we had on those two cops when they arrested black men. We were both afraid for the safety of the driver, and the boy on the bike had been seen and released without any serious injury.

"Later, I told you what the family had heard the cops say to Allan as they slammed him against the hood of the car. 'You hit a white kid. Your black ass needs to be dead.' I repeated to you that I had been advised that the victim had been taken to the hospital and released."

I'll never forget what he said then. "I'm not losing my job defending you."

I knew then that this was not an ordinary action.

"I don't understand, Chief. When Mayor Otis met with us about who would be chief and who would be deputy chief, you said, 'If you support me on being chief, I will support you.' Then you said, 'I will always have your back. If you are trying to do the right thing, I'll have your back. If you make a mistake trying to do the right thing – I'll still have your back.' I took that seriously because you even called me 'son.' I believed you."

"Now, settle down, son. It'll be over soon, and you'll be back on the job," Chief said.

I lashed out. "I'm not your damn son! No father would treat his son like that."

With that, I stormed out of his office, stomped down to mine, picked up my belongings, and locked the door. I got into my car in the parking lot and just sat there.

I couldn't believe what was happening.

I decided to call some folks and tell them what had happened.

First, of course, I called Melissa. She is a stoic, solid woman who first said, "Are you okay?" She was calm and unruffled by the news. She knew the chief, both personally and from talk I would bring home. She couldn't imagine he would turn on me.

Next, I called Anthony Hill; he was in a delicate situation. He was an officer in the TPD and had to walk a fine line between knowing what was actually going on and being able to do something about it. He did say he was there for me. And I know he was. He mostly focused on letting the community know what was going on. This included people like Councilwoman Nettie Davis – the lone black woman on the city's governing body.

In my quandary, my total confusion about why the chief had taken that path, I guessed Anthony's advice was good. I was just speechless. I had had an outstanding record in law enforcement those past nearly twenty years. I was numb.

Chapter Sixteen

The Second Suspension

On July 30, the chief's administrative assistant called me at home. "Chief wants you to meet him in the mayor's office at 1:30p.m."

Finally, I thought. *Finally this thing will be over. He's calling me saying the attorney general's office says there is no case and I'm good to come on back.*

Driving down to city hall, I felt relieved. I could draw a deep breath and look forward to getting back to work. Being off work was not my cup of tea.

When I got into the mayor's office, the mayor wasn't there. I wondered why he had skipped the meeting. He must have had something a bit more important, I guessed. Only the chief and the COO of the city were sitting there when I entered.

I could see their discomfort. The chief was wringing his hands again. The COO revealed an arrogance in his body language that fairly shouted, "You need to be stopped!" Their faces were taut, and suddenly, I became more tense as well.

What was going on?

"You've made a bad choice," the chief began. "You did the wrong thing. We are demoting you to captain."

The COO confirmed what the chief had told me. I couldn't believe my ears.

Demoted to captain?

My office would be moved to the offices of the Police Athletic League, away from the center of action.

These two men were very uncomfortable saying those words about me…challenging me about "making a bad choice" and "doing the wrong thing".

I believe in my heart of hearts that the chief knew good and well that I had done the right thing in the Denton case.

My mind was racing. I, who was responsible enough to make a call that someone should be killed, wasn't smart enough to make the call in a DUI in a hit and run? With nearly twenty years of experience and a great deal of specialized training, I wasn't smart enough to recognize the danger a young black man would be in with an officer who had been written up already for racist responses in minority cases? I, who had a nearly perfect major felony conviction record, with only one case not solved?

Plus, management science and leadership had been my specialty at the FBI academy. When I had the five officers at Hardee's, myself, and the concerned family, that was a very difficult decision situation. I had to think of the liability of the city, but also watch for the civil rights of the victim, the suspect, and the officers who I was protecting, too. Crisis situations can quickly spin out of control. I had to make the right decision, and I had to make it quickly.

While I was having to make quick decisions, the folks who were against me had had a good deal of time to analyze and to tear apart those choices.

I was also aware of my rights under the Constitution. With calm resolution, I stared the chief right in the eyes as I said, "I'm filing a grievance."

The chief responded in a very threatening tone of voice.

"You don't want to do that!" he said. "You just take the demotion, and in six months or so we will have you back at deputy chief."

Yeah, right, I thought to myself.

I truly knew at that time that everything Cliff had warned me about, everything that Marvin Brown, my first mentor on the force, had told me those many years ago – it was all true. When you get to the point where a black man is giving white officers orders, things can go awry. That evil jealousy creeps into a man's soul and begins to take control.

I got up and left without another word. Outside, I called Jim Waide, my lawyer, and told him what was going on. He told me to get over there right away, and we immediately started drafting the grievance hearing document declaring we disagreed with the action.

Jim sent in the paperwork quickly, and a date was set for the hearing: three weeks from the date that they sent the letter.

I was then told that someone had moved the date another two weeks out. The opposition had five extra weeks to create their case against me. After notice of the date change, I never heard another word about that hearing. It was never held, and nothing ever came of that filing.

A few days later, I took my children Marissa and Brandon down to TPD to help me move my stuff to the PAL Building. We walked into the offices and past the chief's office, where he stood leaning against the door frame. Marissa was 4, and Brandon was 14.

At that age, my son was beginning to understand some of what was going on, but my daughter was clueless. Why was this man who was their "office granddaddy" treating their daddy like this? Why was he being so mean to their daddy?

After that move, I took on the captain's role in the offsite office in the PAL Building alongside the Police Athletic League that I had helped to create. With no pay.

Robert's living room

Chapter Seventeen

Harassment and Depression Set In

Our den was suddenly engulfed in a very bright light. It was coming from the parking lot across the street.

Next thing I knew, those pickup lights went out.

As I looked out the window, I could see a pickup in that lot, facing my house. It was about 150 feet away from my window.

The Ku Klux Klan: those white supremacists who have been killing black folks like me for centuries. The ones who some say are still lynching black men in Mississippi and calling it suicide. Still in the 21st century, there are those who hate me for the color of my skin.

A KKK guy in his satin hood and cape had been appearing on YouTube, saying he had to come down to Tupelo and straighten me out. He called me by name. And these guys across the road were part of that effort, I'm sure.

I don't really know if these guys were card-carrying, dues-paying members of the Ku Klux Klan, but they sure did act like it.

They just faced my house, and then they turned off their headlights and sat.

And they sat.

The purpose of just sitting there – across from my home – was to intimidate me. Scare me out of my wits.

And when they did come, my heart started pounding like a jackhammer, and I sweated like it was 110 degrees in the shade.

I sat on the couch with my head in my hands and I began to pray. "God, please protect my precious family! Keep my sleeping family from harm. Hold Melissa, Terrell, Brandon, and Marissa in your arms, safe from these racist folks. Help me protect them."

I thought to myself, *I'm so fed up with this stuff! They'll not get past me. Dear God, I'm not going to just sit here like a duck in a pond. I'll not go down quietly. I'm gonna go out and watch them! Two can play that game.*

"God, please be with me."

They were still there, sitting in their pickup. Staring at my house.

But I had got a plan, too. I knew what I was going to do. I'm no dummy.

Get the rifle. Get in a better place than I am right now. Get where I can see them, but they won't know I'm there – watching them!

Being a cop, I had long ago learned how to get around without making a noise. I quietly got up and unlocked the gun safe on the wall. I pulled out my favorite rifle – the one that would let me zero in on them with the sights.

I headed down the hall and out the back door, dodging the furniture and that creak in the floor just before the back door. My route was well planned out because I had been thinking about this. I had to watch them like they watched me so they couldn't surprise me.

"God, please keep that dog sleeping so he won't wake up and start barking."

At the corner of the house, I put my head real close to the brick to see that they were still there.

They hadn't budged.

It was a moonlit night, and our yard offered a lot of places where my dark silhouette could get lost...small groups of woods, the fence of the dog pen, dark corners where no light existed.

I waited until the moon went behind a cloud and ran to the tall hardwood tree line that formed the border of our property. I moved stealthily along that bunch of trees, making sure I was blending in with them. My eyes were on the distant fence post, where I knew I could watch them, but they couldn't see me.

By the time the cloud moved on, I was near that post. I could always hunker down there and watch. It was just next to a huge anthill.

I was careful not to stand in it. I didn't need a bunch of swarming ants crawling up my legs while I was on "lookout". Besides, they needed to be protected, too, so they could be ready to work tomorrow.

I watched for what seems like hours.

I slid my hand down my leg to make sure the rifle was still there – right where I could grab it and pull it up to my eyes.

It was.

At times, my eyelids slid over my eyes, until I snapped them back up so I could see. The time went by slowly. But I was there, and I was not moving.

They sat for that long, too, these white supremacists. I didn't know who they were by name, but I sure recognized the actions of a racist. Then, at some preordained time, they pulled out with their headlights on, and I sneaked back home the same way I got there, grateful that I had never had to use my gun.

The ants were safe again.

My family was safe.

And I was mad as hell at this situation.

I was sweating, struggling in the dark. I was afraid, but I couldn't remember why.

I woke up to Melissa's voice. "Robert! Robert! You're having another nightmare." And she was right – I had more than a few times when I would wake up from the depths of fear from the events since May 28, 2006.

I slowly opened my eyes to the safety of our bedroom. The digital clock glowed with its eerie numbers: 2:47 a.m.

She was right. It was another nightmare. Just another of many I had nearly every night – horrors that showed up again and again.

It wasn't until years later that I realized I was suffering from PTSD. Many veterans I've met have experienced this same kind of trauma.

All I knew then was that I was afraid. I rolled over and tried to go back to sleep.

After a restless night, I rose to yet another day in this living nightmare of being suspended from my job without a salary. I was frequently shamed on the front page of the newspaper in the county I had lived in for all my forty years. And I had a loving wife, three kids, a house payment, and a car payment.

It was another week of not knowing what the future would hold.

Another month of seeing my life – my successful, orderly, law-enforcing life – fly into the wind like the flames that had consumed my six friends when I was a kid.

I helped Melissa get the kids ready for school, and she went off to work. I watched the sun rise high in the sky.

And I watched the clock in the living room – another one with those eerie green numbers – click, click, click. One minute at a time. All day.

I sat in the chair and cried hopelessly. "Help me, God. Help me."

Yes, I suffered nightmares at night, but what I was living wasn't much better.

I couldn't go anyplace downtown – not to the grocery, to the movies, anywhere – without being recognized. I felt ashamed and embarrassed, and I didn't want to go anywhere anyway.

Everything I had worked for was gone. I have no salary, no job, no respect from anyone. And what would my boys think of me? I was sure they would see me as the hero who climbed Mt. Everest and then slid all the way past the bottom into the depths of disaster.

There's nothing to live for if you can't be a man in your own eyes.

There was a bright spot, however, in those dark days. An anonymous citizen kindly paid my gym fee for six months that summer. I at least had that, but as things got worse in the fall, I stopped going there, too.

Paranoia began oozing into my mind. Who could I trust? Certainly not the coworkers I had thought were my friends, except for Cliff. I just didn't know.

One day a plain white envelope appeared in the mailbox. I stared at it, wondering if it was a threat to my life. Was it threatening Melissa or the kids? It seemed innocent enough; I could feel that it was not fat – no bomb inside – but could it be that white powder that could kill me?

A few weeks before, John Oxford, a community leader in Tupelo, had called me and said a bunch of "powers that be" had gotten together secretly to discuss my situation.

"This deal with Robert Hall is wrong – just wrong", they had said.

"We cannot stop the injustice, and we can't come out publicly against them. But we just can't have Robert leaving the area. He is too valuable as a bridge between the races. His family cannot suffer for these injustices. We've got to do something."

Oxford had explained that sometime soon, they would send me some money to help.

Could this envelope be from that group of folks? Or was it from the ones who were out to hurt me and my family?

I took a deep breath.

I was scared to open it, but I carefully pulled my finger along the edge of the envelope. It was a folded piece of plain paper, and when I unfolded it, a check for $6,000 fell out.

"Cuse me, God... Is this really made out to me?" I looked again. Yes, made out to me, Robert E. Hall.

And signed John Oxford.

Nothing like this has ever happened to me before.

It wasn't a one-time thing, either. For close to a year, those checks came once a month and kept me and my family safe and comfortable when I was working for nothing from the TPD.

There were others, too. The guy at the wellness center who sent a four-figure check from he and his wife. The anonymous envelope on the window of my car, full of hundreds of dollars in cash.

I owe my life to these incredible white Northeast Mississippi folks who helped sustain me through the darkest days of my life.

Interestingly, I didn't get support from the wealthy black community in Tupelo. Even the leaders at my church ignored my situation. I felt they were trying to keep their heads down – to avoid becoming a victim of the same persecution I was facing.

Those Tupelo leaders saved my life.

The depression engulfed me. I had lost 25 to 30 pounds. But I at least had the courage to go to the doctor and have him prescribe some meds for me. I didn't want to sink any further.

But I did. Sometimes the meds helped, and sometimes they didn't.

How had this happened to me? I reran my life day after day. Where had I gone wrong?

Sometimes I got in the car and drove to the church parking lot. I just sat there, talking to God – being angry with God. Should I have taken my chances that Allan would be hurt in the process of getting to the jail? Should I let the cops who had (reportedly) slapped Allan up against the hood of the car just arrest and process him and pray for the best? What might they have done to him?

I spent a lot of time being depressed. I'd never been in a situation like this before, and I didn't know how to handle it. Sometimes I would drive on out to the cemetery to talk to Dad.

I was glad Dad never lived to see the humiliation I experienced during those days. The *Daily Journal* printed my picture every time there was the slightest new event in the case.

I was embarrassed – not only for Melissa and the kids, but also for my entire family.

My dad was a great example of what it means to be a man. He was a deacon at the church, and he was a hard worker at the Purnell's Pride chicken factory. When he was done cleaning up the place, you could eat off of that floor. He was a fine father.

To be a good man, a good father, and a good husband means that you take care of your family – bring home money to feed them, house them, make sure they are healthy and educated. You establish a set of values that show respect for others as well as yourself.

Visiting the cemetery

He taught me how to be a man.

That's not easy in the black world of poverty that many black men find themselves in today. But growing up, I felt loved, protected, and "rich as Rockefeller." When I got a cap gun for Christmas, I thought I was in seventh heaven. When I went to kindergarten in my plaid jacket and dress shirt just like Daddy's and my new-to-me shoes, I felt some kind of cool.

I had no idea I was poor.

What I did know was that I had to live up to my daddy's image. This was what a man was, and I had to be just like him. I even wanted to be a deacon like he was.

I wanted a good job, a happy family with a beautiful wife, and smart kids. Well, I had done that, but now I was a failure.

I had felt loved and secure all my life. That's what a loving family had created for me.

Momma and Daddy both worked and made a living that, while not always stretching as far as one might hope, did cover the necessities: food, clothes, housing. We always went to church where most members were kinfolks.

I can tell you now I needed God to get through all this, and while I didn't understand – and still don't – why these things were happening, my faith in God kept me going.

I have always felt God had a job for me because I "wasn't supposed to be here" since Momma was taking birth control pills. She was supposed to die early and didn't.

So both of us felt touched by God and believed we were on earth for a purpose. She would say to me, "You want to be like these kids here – not like your brothers."

She gave me a couple of other good pointers in life which I have always followed:

"Keep God in front. Look people in the eye. Lots of times, all you have is your word."

I didn't always know what she meant by looking folks in the eye and that all I had was my word. But as I got older, I realized that when you look people in the eye, they respect you. When your word is your bond, folks respect you. In the South when you say, "Yes, sir," and "No, sir," people respect you for it.

I still keep Sunday for Church, and my children do, too. It has not only been a haven in times of trouble, it has also given me a moral foundation. It is a place for joyous occasions, and the place where I found my wife.

Other happy days thoughts included memories of Dad collecting cans to fund my car when I went to college, and the "hog killin'" days.

Each time I drove over to the graveyard, when I turned into the church lot nearby, I'd pass the "hog killin'" tree.

I never passed that tree without thinking of those happy days.

Past that old tree, I'd come to Daddy's grave. I'd stand, and I'd talk to him.

"Daddy, I'm so sorry for letting you down. I didn't do all those things they said I did, because that's not what you and Momma taught me." Often, I would cry because I didn't know what to do.

I'd remember when I first felt like I was "chosen" to be a cop – someone who would help old people and kids, and women, too – folks who were weaker than others. People like Huzzie and Gertie and their mom; people like the six kids that died in the fire. Folks who were vulnerable to the "bad guys".

I had always tried to do the right thing, though – I was fair, even to the suspects I took in. I was fair to the ones I knew for sure were guilty, too, because they were my brothers in the human race, and God would want me to treat them with dignity.

I'd talk to Larry too, a space away from Daddy. "Why did you live that life? Why were you so mad all the time? Why did you have to die so young?"

There between Daddy and Larry was an empty burial lot. Just waiting for someone to fill it up.

Would it be for me?

I'd go back to the car near Dad and Larry's graves and wonder why God was doing this to me. What would I do next?

The hog killin' tree

Sometimes when I was back at home, I'd plot how to get even with the guys that had done me wrong – the guys who had blatantly lied about me and never looked back. I would never *really* act on that, though. It wouldn't be in my soul to do anything like that. But I'd be a liar if I said I never thought of it.

And more than once, I planned my suicide. If God was going to be so mean to me, I would just take my own life. I even figured I'd be buried in that spot next to Daddy and Larry.

I'll get my Glock out of the drawer, slip it into my pocket, and head out for the woods behind our home. I'm not going to mess up our home – that precious home where Melissa and I have made a wonderful life. Where our three kids have grown from children into young adults with the world ahead of them. No, I'm not going to mess up that sacred home and make someone have to clean it up afterward… I remember that first suicide call I went out on… Nobody should have to clean up those parts of folks they loved.

And the minute I thought of those things, I would recall Melissa saying to me, "I'm so afraid that I will come home from school one day and I'll find you dead."

And I had promised her, "I'd never do that to you."

So, it was an exercise in futility. I would never take my own life – the one that God gave me.

Sometimes in my darkest hours, I began to think about who I am and where I came from. My mind wandered to centuries ago.

I could close my eyes and see many black bodies – my ancestors being snatched away from their homes in Nigeria. I had no idea which century they came, but sometime after the 1600s they were kidnapped. I could almost hear those heavy shackles rattle as they swayed in the rough and angry seas that took them far away from their homes. I couldn't even imagine the fear in their hearts at leaving their loved ones.

I felt their nakedness when they had to climb up on slave blocks and were poked to see if they were "fit" enough for purchase.

I was being "poked" to see if I was good enough to be a cop in Tupelo, Mississippi.

I envisioned those people as they dragged themselves through the dusty roadways on the way to the fields.

I was shamed forever.

Emotional chains can be just as heavy as those my ancestors wore – those irons of physical imprisonment, of social isolation, of being cast out from your family. Their chains kept them in bondage all their lives.

Would my imaginary chains do the same?

But, somehow, they had survived. If they could endure and persist, if they could stay alive to father other generations that led to me, well, I guessed I could get through this.

Chapter Eighteen

The Town Gets into It

By the second week in October, my story had been splashed all over the pages of the local newspaper. I was the bad black cop that had protected one of his own instead of agreeing to arrest him after a hit and run.

The city council was mired in these racial issues between the NAACP and the citizens of the city of Tupelo. The council decided to have a meeting to "clear the air" and get the citizens' opinions of these divisive problems.

The meeting was set for Thursday, October 12, 2006.

It was a normal fall night in the South. Temperatures were still warm and the sun set slowly in the west, but at meeting time, it was close to dark.

I won't repeat all that Cliff said, but the main points were that I was being persecuted for the simple reason that I am black. He reiterated my successes in the department and further explained that even he had experienced bias with official investigators, and blamed it largely on his friendship with me. After that meeting, he wasn't surprised to find out that such behavior has ramifications, even if you are white.

I so admired his bravery, and his courage to stand in front of the city council and other citizens, calling for truth. Unfortunately, it turned out to be a life-changing event for him, too.

At the time he spoke out for me, Cliff was the TPD Internal Affairs officer and, as such, had acted within the lines of his job description in making inquiries with the families involved in the Allan Denton incident.

However, when we returned from the community policing conference, he was forbidden to deal with that case at all.

It was no accident that they kept both of us away from any of the official documents connected with that case – specifically victim's records from the hospital. All I ever knew of the victim's injuries were the words of the dispatcher and supervisor on the night of the incident. "The hospital says, 'His injuries are such that he will be released after they have been dealt with.'"

And Cliff's speech didn't go unnoticed by the administration of the TPD.

On November 7, the chief of police removed Cliff Hardy from his position as Internal Affairs investigator and reassigned him to public relations to the Tupelo Apartment and Housing Authority patrol. Cliff's new assignment was in an area of town known to be quite dangerous. Some folks feared for his life, especially if others were called to assist him. They could perhaps take too long to get there, and Cliff would be in serious trouble.

Four days later, Cliff tendered his retirement, effective May 1, 2007. He had accrued sufficient leave time that he was not required to work until the effective date of his retirement.

February 1, 2008, Cliff filed a lawsuit alleging that the city of Tupelo had constructively discharged him in retaliation for his speech, in violation of Title VII and the free speech provisions of the First Amendment.

Yep, Cliff took them to court. Sometimes I wished I had some of his spit and vinegar in me.

Jim Waide was his lawyer. And in the end, it paid off. Jim came out of that trial and told me, "Robert, that was your case in there, and you won this time."

Jim argued that Cliff had been mistreated and put on a dangerous assignment with no partner, where trouble was known to happen and with little expectation of immediate help, should he need it.

The civil case paid off, too. Loss of salary – $100,000; mental anxiety – $200,000. Even without what he paid his attorney, he got a tidy little sum, plus his pension.

He retired to his farm outside of the city and has not been involved in the community since.

I miss him.

Another thing that occurred while all the legal stuff was going on was that the City wanted to know about that "ethics" thing.

While all of this was going on, the city of Tupelo decided to get an outside opinion on their ethics. The city called Trautman, the ethics expert who Cliff and I had brought in to teach the police force about working ethically. They wanted him to evaluate the entire administration of Tupelo.

Trautmen came out and met with the city officials, and they outlined what they wanted him to do.

All the departments – not just the police department, but all the departments – were to be studied.

Trautman did not personally conduct the work in Tupelo, but he recommended a colleague he trusted, Cindy Brown.

Brown requested papers that would help her with the main purpose of the study: "to assess the departmental strengths and deficiencies to develop recommendations for improvement."

She would also include "assessments of cultural diversity among city personnel to identify any challenges to the acceptance of cultural diversity within that population and to gain a better understanding of what is needed to improve cultural relations between the city and the community."

It was a powder keg just waiting for a light.

Suffice to say it was not an easy task. Miscommunication was common between the researchers and the city personnel. Opinions about the purposes or results of the report were often challenged, and there were plenty of articles in the paper about the issues.

While the report was supposed to be completed quickly, nearly two years passed between the call for this action at the city council meeting in September and October of 2006, and the completion of the formal report in September 2008.

And when that report came out, it was not favorable to two departments in the city of Tupelo. While the majority of the city departments came out good, the police department and the utilities department reflected racist cultures.

Chief among the facts presented in the report was evidence of favoritism in awarding work to white-owned employers when black-owned businesses were the ones the council originally selected for the work. At one point, an administrator promised to change that, but they never did. In addition, there were cartoons that turned up during the report investigation that showed racial minorities in foolish positions. The investigators even found two typed pages making fun of the intellect of blacks. There was a letter complaining about AIDS and a "nigger" application for a job. They were all humiliating.

And all these documents had to pass under the noses of the department heads.

There was clear evidence of overt racism happening inside the Tupelo Police Department.

The response to this report was polarizing. The newspaper and many city administrators challenged the validity of the report. They challenged Cindy Brown's work, claiming she hadn't accurately reported the truth of the situation.

Others in the city supported it. In the end, it did not result in massive change.

Tupelo is a wonderful community and a place I am proud to be from. But even in good places like this, once in a while, the bad guys win.

Chapter Nineteen

New Charge

I had just gotten settled in as a captain near the Police Athletic League offices when the TPD came back and said they had "new evidence". Now the Highway Patrol was going to take over the investigation.

This seemed to me to be a way for my opponents to manipulate the justice system. The people who wanted me out of office knew that the police department and the county couldn't get anywhere on their own. They had no evidence to support their claims that I had done anything wrong, and the state had looked at the case and refused to support their accusations. By moving my case into the Highway Patrol's jurisdiction, they would gain important political sway. All they had to do was produce some excuse to move the case.

I never knew what that "new evidence" was, but this time the charge I was facing was perjury.

Perjury! I would lie under oath? I was stunned.

How could these people who knew me even consider that as a charge?

I felt like I was in a different world. I had lived a Christian life since my birth. I had spent my childhood trying to help older people. I dreamed of being in law enforcement so I could keep kids and the elderly from being abused, beaten, killed, or hurt in some other way. I had spent my life trying to always do the right thing, and now they were accusing me of perjury?

I don't lie. Plain and simple.

On September 9, 2006, the *Daily Journal* carried an article quoting the Attorney General Jim Hood: "We initially commented that our investigation was complete. However, due to subsequent information, we are working with the district attorney's office to reevaluate the Hall case."

As a part of the "new" case, I was asked to take a polygraph test.

My lawyer, Jim Waide, felt okay with that. "Just tell the truth," he said. We both trusted that the system would hold and I'd make it through.

It felt like it was no longer about the 14-year-old boy who had been hit. It was about "getting me".

The Highway Patrol would do the polygraph test.

I got up that morning, ready to meet the Highway Patrol polygraph folks whose testing would set me free. I was convinced that my volunteering to take the lie detector test when I didn't have to would prove that I should be back on the force.

So, dressed in pressed slacks, a polo shirt, and, of course, the perfect pair of shoes, I headed out for the Lee County Justice Center where I was to take the tests.

I was really excited – almost like when I went to the mayor's office to meet with the chief and the COO of the City of Tupelo. I just knew this would be the last piece of evidence to prove my innocence.

Certainly no one who knew me could find me guilty of perjury.

I was like a kid going to Disney World.

I'm always early, and this time was no different. I parked and walked up the sidewalk between the imposing tall columns of the Justice Center and through those arched doors. I was met by county folks I had worked with many times before when I was on a case. They greeted me warmly with smiles and handshakes and, "Good to see you." "Sorry this has happened to you." "You'll get through."

I felt okay.

I went up to the second floor, and as I looked left, I peered into the courtroom where I had been for the Darryl Morgan trial. I remembered that district attorney pulling the donut out of his briefcase. It almost made me want to laugh again.

I knocked on the door of the room where I was to take the polygraph. A black guy answered and asked, "Who are you?" I told him, and he seemed a little rattled. I knew I was early, but surely they were prepared. Weren't they?

It was close to 9 a.m. — the time I was to begin the interrogation. I sat down outside the room and waited.

And waited.

And waited.

People were going in and out, very professional-like. People I didn't know. And they were looking at me like, "Yeah, you're the one."

Time went by. I didn't have my watch on, so it was hard to tell how much time had elapsed.

Sometime during that expanse of time, the black guy came out and asked me if I wanted a cup of coffee. "I'm going for one for myself, thought maybe you'd want one, too."

I replied, "No, but thank you for offering."

A white guy came out sometime later and looked at me like I had cursed at him. He wasn't too good at disguising his feelings.

I could see immediately that they were taking the "good cop/bad cop" roles. The black guy was the good one, and the white guy was the bad one.

"We all want to be like you," the black man said in a chatty tone. He looked like the black trustee on a plantation – the guy who was in charge of the slaves. He was trying to be friendly, but it wasn't working: he was like sandpaper…smooth on the top, and yet you just knew he was rough underneath.

And the time was ticking on…we must have been going past ten by then.

What kind of an idiot did they think I was?

Didn't they know I had experience in these kinds of situations? I saw that from the beginning. They needed more tutoring in interview tactics.

The overall goal was to wear me out so I would be confused and say something incriminating. Plain and simple.

But I had the truth on my side.

By this time, it was 11 o'clock and I hadn't even seen the inside of the polygraph room. If they could wear me down and cause me to make errors in what I said, they would win.

I had not had breakfast, nor the coffee, and by then I was beginning to get both hungry and thirsty.

They finally invited me in.

The black guy, who had shaken my hand when he introduced himself, brought the white guy over to me and introduced him. That guy did not shake my hand; he just kept looking sullen and surly.

They offered me the hard chair with the pads in the seat. Those pads are to record the nerves in your buttocks. When you get nervous, there will be measurable twitches that indicate you are lying – or at least ill at ease and not telling the truth.

So there I sat. No one asked me a question at all for 30 to 40 minutes. This interview was supposed to start at 9 and probably be done in an hour or so.

Or so I thought. Melissa got home from work at 3 o'clock. Would I be home when she got there? I was beginning to wonder.

Finally, they put the sensors on my arms at the wrists and the upper torso across my chest.

They asked me simple questions so they could get a reading of my heartbeats when I was telling the truth.

"Is Robert Hall your name?"

"Do you love your wife?"

Then they asked screwy questions like, "Would you like to jump off a building?" (Absolutely not!)

"Do you eat raw steak?" (No.)

They must have had about fifty questions that they were going to ask, and they did. They were the same questions over and over.

"Have you ever lied to anybody?" Now that was a silly question. "Of course." As a teenager, who hasn't lied to their parents on occasion?

They asked about my career and my actions on the night of May 28, 2006.

"Did you call other friends that knew this guy?"

"No, the only friend I called was Chief." That stopped them.

They looked at me.

"Do you work out?"

"I try to keep myself fit." I used to run seven or eight hours a week, but I didn't anymore. However, at that time, I was in pretty good shape, so they decided that my heart rate wasn't registering whether I was lying or not.

By that time, it was after 1 p.m. and I hadn't had a glass of water or any other beverage, any food at all, or a bathroom break.

You might think that these are human rights, but I guessed the polygraph people didn't think so.

It was beginning to wear on me, and it was clear that these guys couldn't get from me what they wanted: mistakes.

Momma always said, "When you are in a situation, you keep God in front of you, and you'll be okay." I remembered those words.

Daddy would say, "A man may not have a penny in his pocket, but if he has a firm handshake and his word is true, he'll get through." He also said, "Look your enemy in the eye."

That's what got me through the ordeal of the polygraph. I would remember my parents' wisdom, and when they asked me a question, I would give a monosyllabic answer. "No." "Yes"

They would respond. "Would you like to expand on that?"

"No, sir, I would not."

It had been so long and the questions were so repetitive that I had memorized the questions and knew which one of them they were asking before they would finish reading it. "Yes," or "No," I'd say.

They would get frustrated because my heartbeat was not only not elevated, it was calm. They couldn't get a liar's reading, and they knew it.

Now what that did was to effectively make the lie detector test invalid. There was no evidence that I had lied at all, and they called the test "inconsistent."

Not worth anything.

When I had been in similar situations as a cop, my goal had been to find the truth. Even suspects deserved to have their Constitutional rights protected. And that polygraph protected mine.

Plain and simple. I told the truth, and they were forced to note that the test was of no real value to their case.

By then, my legs and buttocks had gone to sleep – that chair was hard! My eyelids were heavy. My brain was numb.

But the survival element of my training had kicked in, and the words of my parents had helped, too. SOG officers push themselves to the edge – staying up for days on end, talking to criminals for hours.

And they had been unable to make me mad, either.

I won.

Nothing else was ever said about the polygraph. Except when they decided to ask Cliff Hardy to take one.

They had had such a lack of success with me, they decided to try Cliff. Maybe he'd give them something they could use against me.

So, they made the arrangements for him to come in and get hitched up to the sensors.

Now, Cliff's patience is about a nanosecond long when it comes to injustice. It didn't take five minutes for him to recognize their "procedure" and what they were trying to do. He quickly slung the cords off and told them where to go.

The polygraph incident came up during Cliff's lawsuit against the city.

Jim tore them into shreds on the stands. "How did you get to be on this case?" They would respond, and he would press them on it. He went through the investigative inconsistencies. It was almost pathetic. In fact, Cliff said Jim "cut through their guts and pulled out their livers!"

Good old Cliff. He is a firecracker, and I was glad he was on my side.

I guess the records of our polygraphs went to the "round file" in the Highway Patrol Department after that. Never to be heard from since.

Honest citizens are the ones most likely to fall prey to the justice system. They trust the courts, and they believe in the system. They believe that in the end, truth will out and justice will win. But as I was discovering, the justice system isn't always just, and honest people like me pay the price.

Chapter Twenty

The Grand Jury

There was a saying at the academy and the FBI training center: "You can indict a ham sandwich."

A grand jury – whether federal or state – is selected from the same group of citizens as a regular jury, but these people agree to much longer terms. It is their task to decide, after hearing from the prosecution, whether there is enough evidence to bring the defendant to trial. Because only the state or federal side is presented, (there is no defense evidence presented at all), the members of the jury are often not really in a position to make a fair judgment. That's why you can indict a ham sandwich.

So, the jury's job is simple: they have to decide if there is enough proof to warrant the expenditure of the city, state, or federal government to try this case? They do not decide guilt or innocence; they just determine if the case is solid or not based on what the prosecutorial side presents.

Oftentimes if blacks get called to be on a grand jury, they don't want to serve. In my experience, African-Americans often are afraid to be on a mostly white panel, so they look long and hard to find a way out of serving. That means in states like Mississippi, you can almost guarantee a majority white jury. At least that's what my attorney thought.

This time was going to be different, though. We both had confidence in the system. Jim Waide and I decided that my case was conclusive and that our legal system would be totally fair. I would appear to testify on my own behalf.

Truth would win.

So, in dealing with the grand jury and a charge of perjury, I pled "not guilty".

Jim said, "Go ahead and testify to the grand jury. Get it thrown out. Then you can get on with life."

In the aftermath of these events, I think Jim blamed himself for my being charged.

The grand jury hearing date was set. In the meantime, I continued to work for TPD as a captain in the offsite offices in the PAL Building...for no salary.

The day to testify came, and I put on my best clothes so the jurors would know I was a respectable man – a man of honor and an upright citizen.

One of the things I found out was that they changed the charges against Allan Denton. Instead of a simple "hit and run", it was now "DUI maiming" which is a *very serious* crime. It would apply to situations where the victim's arm had been torn off or another serious injury had occurred.

I was told at the Hardee's that night that the boy had been examined and released that same night! Furthermore, in his position as Internal Affairs officer, Cliff hadn't seen any indication that the boy had been *maimed*!

But this change in the charge impacted the charges they were bringing up against me. In addition to obstruction of justice and accessory after the fact, the Highway Patrol Department had added the perjury charge.

There is a thing called "stacking the charges" in law enforcement. It's when the prosecutor asks for additional charges – in this case, perjury – in order to be sure they get the lesser charges.

They were stacking the charges against me.

I waited outside the grand jury room to be called. A circuit court judge I knew passed by me and stopped. "I know what is happening here. I had to recuse myself, because I know what the ruling will be. Hang in there".

It was like I was walking into an ambush. I felt like the jungles of Vietnam surrounded me, and I had no idea that the enemy was hidden and was ready to shoot.

It came my time to testify. I was challenged with the earlier testimony of a white officer who claimed that I had called him eight years before, around 1998, to ask for Allan to be released from custody on a different charge.

I never had any memory of that happening. I had never met that officer, much less had his phone number. To me, it was a lie that was designed to convict me.

The officer who swore to that information said that I was trying to "get Allan Denton off" from something because I knew him. But, interestingly enough, that same officer supposedly also testified that Allan was a "good kid". To this day, I have no idea what the boy was supposedly being held for in that case, why I would want him released, or what happened after that. It is all a mystery to me.

When it came my time to testify, I was nervous as a cat in a room full of rocking chairs. I'd done this many times before, but I'd always been the law enforcement officer, testifying to materials that I had gathered as a detective and willing to indict a person that I knew to be guilty. I wouldn't be there otherwise.

This time, I was the "charged" person. They didn't often come before the jurors. But I was so sure, as was my absent attorney, that the system would support me that I tried not to worry.

Once the prosecutor began to question me, I knew I was in trouble.

This was a man whose home I had guarded when he had been threatened; a man to whom I had presented cases. He knew I was thorough, well prepared, fair and efficient. I was a good cop. But he was trying to make me out to be a hotshot cop flexing my muscles to save a black kid.

He was trying to figure out questions that would trap me, and I knew that. He wanted to intimidate me, to catch me in a lie.

But I don't lie.

"What about the scene of the crime, the hit and run case?" he asked.

"When I drove by it was as quiet as a park. There were no visible tire tracks, no smashed down bushes, no broken twigs. Nobody was there, no one had been there, and as far as I knew, there were no orders to go there."

I had gone to the crime scene, and to my knowledge, *none* of the officers involved that night had been there. There had been no yellow tape to keep the area from being contaminated.

"This is some kid you go to church with isn't it?"

"Yes, sir, but we don't socialize with the family. They are just part of our church."

"What about this kid's 'extreme' injuries?"

"I had no idea, sir" I replied, "because anything concerning this case had been officially kept from me since almost Day One. I have not seen the first record of anything on that case. My responses were quick and accurate."

"Here you are releasing a drunk driver who had just hit a young teenager on a bike and left the scene." I knew Allan was not drunk. The arresting officers had no proof he was drunk. And I had never met or talked to the family or the individual who was hit.

In my mind, the officers who were guilty of being written up for racist activity were more of a danger to the driver. And I simply could not believe that if I told the truth I would be believed. I was absolutely stunned that somehow my word was not seen as the truth.

My parents raised me to have my word as my honor, and I have followed all that all of my life.

"You wanted to protect him, didn't you?" he asked.

"I feared for his life at the hands of the officers that were going to..." He loudly told me to stop my answer and would not let me finish.

In fact, anytime I tried to expand on my fears for the life of the suspect, I was shut up instantly.

Now, if Jim had been there, he could have gotten that information into the trial, but he wasn't there. As I said before, we both believed that justice would prevail, and to this day, he blames himself for my trials.

At any rate, I was not allowed to explain why I took the actions I did.

I answered honestly as best I could.

What I continued to see at every juncture was that there was no real concern for the victim of the crash. It was all an intense effort to get me out of the department.

The boy was just the useful tool they had been waiting for.

The grand jury was made up of twenty people – nineteen whites and one black. Now that in and of itself is not the issue. But later the single black man, a preacher, on the grand jury told me, "You didn't have a chance. That place was so racist, I got up and left. There was no way I could have voted for an indictment."

You know how your mom and dad tell you something important over and over and you ignore it? Then one day, the thing they warned you about happens and bingo… You realize you were wrong and they were right?

This was the day I realized that everything my white best friend, Cliff, told me was true.

So much for the system. That day, in front of the grand jury, I was the ham sandwich.

Chapter Twenty-One

The Indictment

Once the grand jury determines that a case is worthy of spending the county's money on, they send the documents to the judge to sign. The next step is that it is returned to the district attorney, and his work *really* begins.

He has to build his case with more depth than he was able to present to the grand jury, plus write the indictment. Often this is the time that the district attorney and the defense attorneys begin their "give and take" processes – usually called "plea bargaining".

Plea bargaining is the part of the legal system where the Constitutional rights of the defendant and those of the accuser are measured by the two lawyers and they try to come out with a compromise. This is the stage where you have to really have faith in your attorney.

After the grand jury hearing, I found myself in the purgatory of plea bargaining. All my hopes rested on Jim Waide and the negotiating he was doing on my behalf. While Jim had total control of my life, I waited to be indicted.

I still didn't believe what was happening.

"Hey, Robert," Jim said one day when we were together, "I need some help in my office that I think you could provide. You could interview some folks for me and do some research. What do you think?"

I wasn't sure how I could be of help to him, but I imagined he was feeling sorry for me. I decided if he thought I could help, then I'd try. I listened to his rationale.

"Nah," he said when I asked if this was just a pity job. "You are a seasoned investigator and officer. You can bring a perspective I don't have, and I could really use you."

"I'm in," I said. I started showing up at his office, waiting for assignments.

It turned out there really was a place for me, especially as he prepared cases against the city. I helped him protect the civil rights of employees. For instance, if an employee had been fired unlawfully, Jim would take the case, and I would do some of the research. Beyond that, I would review pertinent information.

It really was a pretty good arrangement, and I was grateful to him for the job and his confidence in me.

It was October 29 when my indictment was ready to be delivered. Typically, those papers are carried from the DA's office to the defense attorney's office.

But these were not typical times.

The sheriff had a plan. He knew I was working for Jim, so he decided his officers would burst into the office and handcuff me with the press right there to record it. They were already seeing it on the front page of the paper.

Several uniformed officers threw open the office doors, shouting, "Where's Robert Hall?" The office staff was terrified and answered in shaking voices, "He's out of town, doing work for Jim Waide."

They quietly sulked away, leaving in a really bad mood.

Once served, I would have to show up at the jail, be fingerprinted, and then post bond and be released on my own recognizance.

Ironic, wasn't it… I was in trouble for releasing a suspect to his own recognizance, and now I would be released on the same thing.

I had a friend at the jail. He called me, promising to let me know when he knew they would be arriving with the indictment so I could come right in earlier.

He called, and I drove over to the jail.

I pulled the car into the parking lot – a little further away from the entry than usual, so as not to be recognized. I ran in through all the rain that had just begun, signed the papers, presented bond, and went out to my car.

No big deal.

Just as I got in the car, I saw the newspaper's reporter pull up. He was the same one who had been at Jim Waide's office ready to photograph the officers bursting in and arresting and handcuffing me. He jumped out of the car in a big rush, and just about that time, a gust of wind came up and his hat blew off into a puddle. He reached down to get that and dropped the camera in the same puddle. He was frustrated, angry, and dripping wet, with a wet camera and wet hat.

I smiled to myself, pulled out of the lot and slowly headed home.

Robert and Melissa

Chapter Twenty-Two

In Limbo

During the months of November, December, January, and most of February, the attorneys were wrangling back and forth about my case. Trial or no trial? Plead guilty or plead innocent? If I agree to this, can you agree to that?

What will I do?

The holidays came and went, and my life went on, but that holiday spirit couldn't pierce my depression about my situation.

I later found out that a number of good people – largely white businessmen – in Tupelo had combined to secretly support me when the grand jury handed down their opinion.

Jack Reed, Sr., called me sometime in February. Now, Jack was a "leader of leaders" in Tupelo. Not only did he own one of the largest retail stores in the town, but he also ran for governor in the late '90's. Nothing happened in the area that Jack didn't know about. And he was a kind, intelligent Southern gentleman who was respected all over the nation. When Jack called, you went.

"David Rumbarger wants you to call him," he said.

"Why?" I asked.

"He may have something for you," he replied.

"Has he read the newspapers for the last six months? Doesn't he know what's happening to me?" I couldn't believe he wanted to talk to me.

"Just call him," Jack said.

So, I called the Community Development Foundation, where David was the executive director. This organization was created by George McLean, the publisher of the local newspaper, and others to kind of replace a traditional Chamber of Commerce. It has been an immense success and is studied by communities all over the world.

David answered the phone when I called. "I'd like to see you. Do you have a time that would be good for you?"

We set it up, and I put that meeting on my calendar.

When the time came for our appointment, we sat down in his office.

"I'd like to hire you immediately," David told me. He named a salary that was well beyond that of a cop. "I have a special place for you – one that only you can fill."

With that, he offered me a job as director of community engagement, helping to facilitate the incentives Toyota agreed to when they selected our area for a site for a new car production plant. CDF and Three Rivers Planning and Development District pulled together to get the counties of Lee, Pontotoc, and Union to cooperate so they could make Toyota "an offer they couldn't refuse". It would change the economics of our part of the state immeasurably. Here was my chance to be a part of it.

Now, I'm not naïve. Part of my value to the city was that I could breach the racial chasm and get respect in both areas. Certainly, Toyota would not want to be building their factory in a town that was mired in a racial conflict. If they hired me to help secure the Toyota plant, that would be a big success!

I was breathless. Clearly, he didn't have any problems with my charges or the perception that I was partial to blacks. I had to think things over.

Should I plead guilty to the charges and hope I could get by with suspended sentences? Should I face the trial – whenever that might come – and make my family pay the price again of all the publicity?

I went home to discuss it with Melissa. She was my rock and my anchor. I would need to see what she thought.

Lee County Justice Center

Chapter Twenty-Three

In Court

When, in early March, David Rumbarger offered me a better paying job and a return to "normalcy" for me and my family, it raised a whole new set of questions. What would it cost me to plead guilty versus not guilty?

On the plus side, if I pled not guilty, I would clear my name forever. I would be found innocent, and the racism that was permeating the department toward me at that time would, hopefully, vanish. My wife and my kids could hold their heads up high. They could join me in being proud of what I had done because I had been right!

Jim Waide was chomping at the bit for me to give him the go-ahead to tear into the administration and their case against me.

On the minus side, I could draw a 100 percent white jury – Jim warned me of that – and perhaps be found guilty. Who knew how long a sentence I might be given? It would not be easy if that were the case.

If I pled guilty, on the plus side, I would be able to go on with my life. I would spend the forthcoming years endeavoring to overcome the terrible reputation I now had among many of the citizens of Tupelo and Lee County. With the CDF offer, I would be making quite a bit more than I would as a cop.

On the negative side, I would have a record. I would be a convicted felon. Not exactly what I had had in my "I want to be..." column in the high school yearbook.

The attorneys were at work. The DA and Jim went back and forth. The City really didn't want to put me in jail. Yeah, some of the officers in my department would have probably liked that, but it wasn't mandatory. They mostly wanted me out of a job.

By late February, the legal teams seemed to be in agreement. The plan was for us to plead guilty to reduced charges: misdemeanors of obstructing justice and accessory after the fact; no perjury. I would face a suspended sentence of one year and a small fine.

Melissa and I talked about it, but, as you might expect, she left the decision to me.

I tossed and turned and lost sleep, but finally decided that the immediate needs of the family mattered above all. At least we could move on with our lives with this decision.

A part of me will always hate that I didn't stand and fight, but another part of me recognizes that any husband and father must consider the needs of his family first.

Funny, isn't it… I tell the truth, and I get arrested for a felony. I tell a lie by pleading guilty, and I get a good job, making more money than I was before.

Go figure.

It was early spring, and the day of reckoning had arrived. While I knew what I had to do, I didn't want to. But it seemed the only way out.

I dressed professionally and told Melissa that if she went, I probably wouldn't plead guilty because I was still so furious at the entire situation, I could hardly speak of it.

She was to go on to school, and I would tell her all about it when she got home.

I drove down in the freshness of the morning and met Jim in his office. I sat there while lawyers did their thing. It was almost like a game – "I'll do this if you'll do that." Back and forth. Soon it was time, and we headed over to the courthouse.

When Jim and I walked into the courtroom, most of the players were already there, including the sheriff and the chief. No one would look me in the eye; I could tell they were all ill at ease. In addition to the chief and sheriff, there were the white cops that Cliff had investigated. They all knew their case was weak, I believed, but here we were.

The clock ticked on. The tension in the room was so thick, you could have cut it with a knife. Finally, it was "case time."

The bailiff announced the entrance of the judge, and we all stood up. Those black gowns and the audience standing in silence relayed respect. The judge sat down first.

"You may be seated," he said as he sorted out some papers. All the folks shuffled their papers and materials, then sat down in the pews and waited.

I could see the chief from the corner of my eye. He was wringing his hands, as he always did when he was nervous. The sheriff's eyes were riveted on the judge. No one over there looked comfortable.

The judge banged his gavel on the wood base with a loud thud. That sound rang through the room, and we all knew the time had come.

This was it.

Would I fight for truth against what I believed were lies from their side? Or would I cave and lie about my own "guilt"?

The judge cleared his throat and asked me to stand. He read the charges.

"You have been charged with two misdemeanors: obstruction of justice and accessory after the fact. How do you plead?"

"I plead not guilty, Your Honor."

An audible buzz ran through the audience. The pencils and pens of the media began to scratch on their pads.

"Then, why are we here?" the judge asked.

"I am here because I know what they are going to say I did. But those white officers are against me. I don't believe I have a chance in a court of law because everything has been denied me. You have the access to the records; I have not had the opportunity to study the reports or the evidence. That has been denied me. Everything has turned against me.

"I have a family, and these people have turned the court against me. I want it on the record now: this cannot be a fair case!"

Jim had coached me well in how to make this statement. It would ensure that it was on the record that I felt the case was skewed.

"So, how do you plead?" asked the Judge again.

"Guilty," I said.

I was given a suspended sentence of one year, and a fine of $500.

I walked out of there, convicted of two misdemeanors, rather than felonies (thanks to Jim). But I still had a record.

No matter, when I left the courtroom, I felt like a weight had been taken off my shoulders. I had protected my family's identities and economic stability, I still could walk downtown in Tupelo, and equally important, there were people in my world who believed in me.

They knew what kind of man I was, and those who didn't yet know would come to discover who I was. That year of bad publicity did not speak for the real Robert Earl Hall, in my opinion.

I was free again, but I was no longer a cop.

Home of CDF in 2007

Chapter Twenty-Four

Community Development Foundation

The very next workday, I walked up the steps of the old post office on Main Street and into my new world. Inside, folks walked around the rooms in business casual clothes – no blue uniforms. Unlike specific offices in the TPD, there was no Confederate flag, nor was there a stuffed black bear hanging by a noose in the corner. There was no undercurrent of "I'm black, and you are white."

I was greeted by a smiling woman who promptly called Barbara Smith, Vice President of Chamber Services, from her office.

"Robert Hall has arrived."

Out she came, extended her hand, and said, "Welcome to CDF." And off we went. She took me under her wing and did the introductions, then led me to my own cubicle. My "next door neighbor", Gena Black, was a white woman who became a very special friend.

I've never had "black friends" and "white friends". I have "friends", and she was the first one of many there at CDF.

CDF serves as the economic heart of Tupelo, running business development seminars, offering networking opportunities, holding community leadership classes, and recruiting new businesses like Toyota to the region.

I think my value to CDF and Tupelo was that I reached across the race barrier and communicated with citizens of all colors in our town. In the latter years at the TPD, I had often been in public situations where I had to relate to both rich and poor, black and white, and educated and uneducated. I just saw them as people, and I soon got used to speaking to folks as human beings. I knew community policing, too. I truly believed in *knowing* the folks I served. Beyond that, I was easily recognized in the area. Thanks to all the publicity I had received with rank advancements, my successful arrests, and being sent to the FBI Academy, my face had been in the *Daily Journal* often. I also grabbed coffee and met downtown with folks a lot. I like people.

I think that reaching out to all the citizens in Northeast Mississippi was what they wanted me to do at CDF.

The truth is that communications between blacks and whites can be difficult. Neither group fully understands the prevailing culture of the other, and consequently they often talk past each other.

I would connect the community to whatever it was that CDF was doing at the time.

CDF taught me more than I could ever have imagined. David Rumbarger was a classic mentor who was able to listen, question, and teach all at the same time.

It was just his leadership style, and I loved it.

Every Monday morning, David would meet with members of his team.

"What's going on in your area?" he would ask. Often, there were really good responses. They could be new ideas or follow-up on things that my colleagues had in progress. Sometimes a few members would be rather quiet, with little or nothing to offer. "Nothing new, David."

Too many of those answers and that person would not be attending the meetings anymore.

My first lesson, then, was to always be thinking. Always have action plans in the works. And here was where David became a fantastic mentor.

I'd have read something or gone out into Tupelo and discovered a particular need or a place where our services could fit with what might help that area be a better place.

When I piped up with my new idea, David would press me with the "Why? What? When? How? Who?" questions. If I didn't know the answer, I'd have a chance to search it out before the next meeting. He was always open to ideas. Yet, he would also say, "Go back to the drawing board." He wanted me to go back and work out the kinks – to polish that idea – and then bring it back to him for consideration.

Chief among my responsibilities in my new job was to listen to black people and encourage them to join in and participate in community activities that would better their lives.

For instance, one of the most important ideas I had was creating a program called Project Elect.

Pretty close to the same time I joined the CDF staff, the counties of Lee, Pontotoc, and Union created PUL, an alliance for community and economic development aimed at providing Toyota with an outstanding location for their next American factory.

That factory would mean incredible economic growth for the area, not only during the creation and building of the factory itself, but also in the number of jobs they would be offering to our qualified citizens. There would be a two- or three-year period during which construction workers in our area would have jobs (and at a great salary, too), and once that was finished, the payroll for operation as the corporation built their Corolla would add an unbelievable number of jobs in the area.

I know how many black folks think. The truth of the matter is we are always way behind in some of these situations.

For one thing, black folks are more likely to rely on a person-to-person approach to getting a job. We tend to show up to a business and ask about a job opening, but today, most of those applications are handled online. And in the case of Toyota, they would have filled any contracts with local businesses months before the factory actually opened.

We blacks just didn't know that stuff.

And even before that, black kids were dropping out of high school more often than the white kids. Like me, they often didn't see college as a real possibility, and some of them even believed the only future waiting for them was being in jail. We needed to reach these kids and encourage them to stay in school and pursue a career after they graduated.

My project was designed to teach black ministers, who are often the most influential members of our community, how things work and what paths kids might have after high school so they could go back to their congregations and pass that information along.

I introduced the idea to Rumbarger, and he asked those questions again and again to make sure the project could work. Then he suggested I go tell Jack Reed, Sr., all about it. Jack was one of the most persuasive people in Tupelo, and when he gave you his "thumbs up," you were in.

I made an appointment to meet with him. On the appointed day, I walked through the Main Street entrance to his store. It was the epitome of the traditional department store – a sense of class in the displays, the products, and the welcoming and friendly nature of the staff. It was always a pleasure to shop at Reed's. You left the chaos and commotion of the outside world and stepped into a peaceful, relaxing environment.

I climbed the stairs in the middle of the men's department and headed toward Jack's office. He was waiting.

Jack is many things, but among them is a classic Southern gentleman. He is gracious to women, as well as men, and he talks with a soft, elegant accent that speaks of time gone by.

"Raw-buht", he said in his calm Southern accent. "Tell me what yo-wuh project is all about."

So, I began. I told him about the exciting proposal I had put together. I listed the black people I would invite to a "planning" meeting where I would lay out the possibilities and how this program might work. I told him how I was just sure this would help bridge the deep gap between the races. We needed to work together to bring blacks up to an understanding that whites already seemed to have.

When I finished, in his slow Southern way, he said, "Now, Raw-buht, I like this idea, and it's a good one, and I appreciate all the work you have put into it".

He drew a longer breath and said, "But one thing you are going to have problems with is the black ministers – you will have infighting."

I was stunned. I couldn't believe what he was saying. *Infighting? These are ministers! We are all black!*

Then he said, "But I don't want you to take my word for it. I want you to go ahead with this meeting, and when you've had it, let's get together again, and you can tell me about it."

I didn't understand that. I was so disappointed in his response. He went on and talked about Dr. King and other black leaders, but my mind was on the reality of what he was saying.

It wouldn't work?

Well, Jack Reed, Sr., I'll show you. I was so confident, I made an appointment with him for the day after the meeting. *I've got you in my sights. We will make this thing work.*

The day came for the meeting, and everyone showed up. These participants represented roughly 1,615 members of black churches in the Tupelo area. All black folks – mostly men, but Nettie Davis was there, as she was a member of the city council. It was important to have her approval for whatever I wanted to do.

I wanted all the churches to work together to try to keep these kids from dropping out of high school and get better jobs in Tupelo.

My PowerPoint presentation was ready. I had worked hard to develop slides on all the important issues we were facing: community development, economic development, education, workforce development, entrepreneurship, existing industry, small business development, community involvement, volunteer programs, health, and crime. I emphasized how the churches would all work together to try to keep these kids from dropping out of high school.

It was colorful. It had data. I had the stats and all that stuff to go with it.

In short, it was dynamite.

Six minutes into the program, the new leader of the NAACP stood up over one of the black ministers and threatened to slap him.

What in the world was going on?

I had noticed there had been some small chatter while I was presenting, but I had had no idea what it was about. Now these two adult men were shouting at each other and threatening to get violent. The room was split: NAACP had their side, the minister had his. Their voices got louder and louder, others joined in, and it was going to explode soon.

Before anyone knew what was happening, the two men headed out of their seats and exited the meeting room, still yelling at each other as they passed down the hall and outdoors to the sidewalk. The audience followed, eager to see what was going to happen.

Uh oh.

Jack Reed, Sr., had been right.

Until we learned to get along with each other, we couldn't hope to get along with the white folks.

I couldn't help but think of Willie Lynch's letter, a famous document in the black community. It was supposed to be written by a slave owner before the Civil War, and it claims to tell other slave owners to pit the blacks against each other – lighter ones against darker ones and so forth. The message Lynch supposedly set forth was that if you can keep the blacks fighting each other, they will be easier to control.

Now, legitimate historians over many decades have discounted the letter as a fake. The dating and other elements are all off, but the message could be true.

Until we can get along with each other, we can never hope to get along with others.

I kept my appointment with Jack and told him what had happened. Then I let that program sit in the closet for nearly a decade.

The Toyota Deal

Once the announcement of the Toyota selection was made publicly, the community development section of CDF was off and running. Everyone in the organization was connected to the Toyota effort in some way…some more so than others.

We put our boots on the ground and reached out to the grassroots community here in Tupelo. We planned trips to Georgetown, Kentucky, where the latest Toyota plant had been built.

It's always a good idea to go learn from folks who do things well, and they had been the winner in the earlier competition to become a Toyota factory location. Their factory was up and running, so we could go learn from them.

I was able to make a couple of trips there – mostly to take city leaders and local businessmen from Tupelo to visit and see how they could most successfully help with Toyota's getting settled in near Tupelo.

I made the arrangements for the journey, and on the appointed morning, we left early. It's close to a seven-hour trek, and we were set to arrive around noon.

As our bus lumbered north, the passengers settled into their own places – some where they could read, sleep, or perhaps even do some work. Others gathered in small conversation groups, trying to decide what to ask of the Georgetown staff who had gone through this before.

They leaned over the seat arms and twisted their bodies to see the folks sitting around them.

"What do you think is the most important thing we should know as we plan for this factory?"

"How much did it cost you to do this?"

"What was the hardest part of absorbing a Japanese company into the Kentucky culture?"

We were met by the Toyota brass, and after a brief but welcome lunch, we were led into a room where they introduced us to our future.

One of the things you must understand about Toyota: There is the Toyota way to do things, and nothing else matters. It is the *only way* in their world. They have been extremely successful and have studied the process of how to manufacture a very good product. They have analyzed to the nth degree how things get done, and if you want to be a long-term Toyota employee, you will follow that way of doing things.

It was a long meeting, full of information on relationships between the car company and the community, the company and its employees, and the construction of the plant. This was a well-thought-out meeting on the Georgetown organization and physical layout. Ours would be similarly designed.

We broke for dinner and a good night's sleep.

On the next day we toured the factory and learned more about the "Toyota Way". They were serious about that. There would be no variations.

After lunch, we boarded the bus and returned to Tupelo, full of new ideas and new ways of thinking. We were ready to share them with members of our community, as well as other business leaders.

It was a good foundation for our newest and biggest industry yet.

Chapter Twenty-Five

They Did It to Themselves

Another of my Toyota pre-opening projects dealt with the security needs that Toyota would have when the plant was completed and cars started rolling off the line.

David walked in one day and said, "Call the Toyota people working in security. They need to start making plans for connecting with the local folks."

CDF works with the local communities in the fifteen-county region of Northeast Mississippi, and getting Toyota to locate in our region was a three-county effort. Whereas most counties are resistant to joining with neighboring areas, the culture developed years ago by George McLean supports the mantra, "a rising tide raises all boats". Thus, in order to get Toyota to come to Tupelo, the counties of Pontotoc, Union, and Lee had banded together to put forth the best offer we could. Their leadership never hesitated to pull together, so the Pontotoc Union Lee (PUL) partnership was effective and well-known in the area. And it worked.

It was important for us to convey to the law enforcement, emergency health responders, and fire departments in that three-county area exactly what it was that Toyota wanted. I was the liaison in that area.

I started by calling our contact in Toyota's security department. When the person on the other end of the phone answered, at first I did not realize who I was talking to. As far as I knew, he was just a guy who knew what we needed to do to get the security section up to speed.

Little did I know he was the director of security for the entire Toyota organization – US, Japan, and all international sites. If I had known, I would have been greatly intimidated!

The director gave me the rundown of the "Toyota Way" to handle this issue. I was to gather all the emergency responders and others together so the Toyota staff could come to Tupelo and discuss their expectations for how the "teams in the trenches" would work with the plant.

I made all the arrangements for the meeting with the Toyota staff and then started making calls to the Tupelo emergency services departments.

Who did I call first? The Tupelo police chief.

"Hey, Chief, how ya doin'?" I asked when he answered the phone. "This is Robert Hall."

The chief was audibly nervous. I could just see those hands wringing.

I continued, "I've been named a liaison between CDF and Toyota, and part of my job now is to set up a meeting with the security team from Georgetown to come and educate our first responders about the 'Toyota Way'. We will be having that meeting two weeks from tomorrow at 10 a.m. here in the CDF conference room. You'll get an invitation card with the particulars on it, but can I count on you and a couple of your officers to be there?"

It was fairly well known that when Toyota came to town, it was like a fairy godmother had flown in. If you cooperated and did things right, you might get a new squad car or fire truck for your community. And Toyota had already pledged $50 million to education in our area. They were quite up front about this: we have good schools, but the Toyota Way wants extraordinary schools. So, we were delighted to receive these funds. In later years, they gave us an extra $10 million. We needed to be nice to Toyota.

Everyone wanted a piece of Toyota.

"We'll be there, Robert."

"Good," I said. "See you." And I hung up, grinning.

No words can express how I felt at that moment. It was like I had just grown a new set of wings. I have my power back, and the chief had to be nice to me if he wanted any kind of good relationship with Toyota.

Next day, Anthony Hill called and asked, "What's this thing about Toyota? Chief called me and a couple of other patrolmen and told us we have to be at CDF at a certain time in a couple of weeks. He tried to downplay his annoyance, but he said it almost grudgingly, like it was a 'required meeting."

My second call was to the sheriff. His response was different than the chief's had been. You'd have thought we were best friends. There was no evidence of the roles he and his staff had played in my recent "change of jobs".

"Sure," he said. "We'll be there."

I finished the calls and sat back in my chair. Only a short while ago, those departments had been instrumental in my removal from office, and now they had to come to a meeting because I had called them.

Isn't that something?

The two weeks went by in a flurry of doing things for the Toyota folks. Before long, it was the morning of the meeting, and I stood at the door, greeting people.

"Welcome." "Glad you could come." "Good to see you." Lots of hand shaking all around.

A table sat in the front of the room, and as the men from Toyota arrived, they were shuffled off to their seats there. David Rumbarger also sat at that table, and surprise surprise, I had a seat there, too.

About forty emergency responders and other attendees sat in the audience, as did the officers from the TPD and Lee County sheriff's office.

And I was at the head table. I can't deny it; there was a small bit of gloating in my heart at that moment.

David stood up first and welcomed everyone. He then introduced the role of CDF and Toyota. He discussed how important this meeting was for our economic development and for building relationships and understanding. We were all part of a team whose goal was to ensure the safety of all areas of the Toyota world outside the factory.

After that, he personally presented the four speakers from the company who had really called this meeting.

But instead of calling them to come up to the podium, David turned to me.

He said, "Let me introduce you to Robert Hall, the director of community engagement here at CDF. He is in charge of the creation of the security section of the PUL Alliance. Robert, come on up."

There I stood. Right in front of the officers who had been part of my downfall.

And now they had to listen to me.

I was nervous.

I had strategized with Toyota to make sure I addressed the things that had to be included, such as how to deal with emergencies in the factory without interrupting the operations, as well as what the proper response to those issues might be.

I covered what they thought I could cover, and then it was time for me to relinquish the stage to the four visitors from the company.

Those folks at Toyota do their homework. When I had been driving them back from the airport, they had quizzed me on some of my background, including the SWAT and SOG teams, the FBI Academy, and other such things.

Well, the first representative from Toyota got up and began.

Only he wasn't talking about the "Toyota Way".

No, he began by talking about me!

I was stunned. He discussed my background and my rise in the TPD. He ran through my credentials and said I understood relationships and building them. He summarized by saying I knew community policing, which went directly to the Toyota philosophy.

At the end of his piece, he added. "We are here for you. If you have any questions, situations, or issues, just call Robert, and he can get hold of us." I cannot imagine what was going through the minds of the TPD and the Lee County sheriff's people right then.

For me, everything they said after that was a blur. All I could think of was that now those officers had to go through me to get anyone at Toyota.

Unlike the officers who had refused to recognize the proper procedure and gone directly to the chief with anything, these guys all had to go through me to get to the head guys at Toyota.

There is some justice sometimes. They had to respect me, like it or not, because I was between them and the brass.

After a couple of hours, the meeting ended, and there was a lot of chatting. And interestingly, many of the law enforcement folks came up and shook my hand. They were smiling, complimentary, and just plain nice.

One chief from Baldwin came up and told me, "Your TPD chief is hating what happened to you, and any of these sheriffs and chiefs would love to have you on their team."

Remember I had been their top officer when this happened. I could only imagine how they felt, sitting there in the audience.

Well, they did it to themselves.

70/59

NORTHEAST MISSISSIPPI

Daily Journal

WEDNESDAY
February 28, 2007
Regional Edition

Volume 133 • No. 334

A LOCALLY OWNED NEWSPAPER DEDICATED TO THE SERVICE OF GOD AND MANKIND.

50 CENTS • TUPELO, MISS.

"We did our homework with site selection. As Elvis would say, 'Only fools rush in.'"

Ray Tanguay, executive president of Toyota Motor North America

"This project is the crown jewel of economic development."

Gov. Haley Barbour

"Today we're laying the cornerstone of the next era in manufacturing excellence in Northeast Mississippi."

U.S. Rep. Roger Wicker, R-Tupelo

Oh, what a feeling!

Sen. Trent Lott, from left, Gov. Haley Barbour and Toyota executives Seiichi Sudo, Gary Convis and Ray Tanguay celebrate the announcement of Toyota's development of the Wellspring Project at the Tupelo High School Performing Arts Center on Tuesday. The company will build its popular sport utility vehicle at the facility. Production of the Highlander at the 1,700-acre site is expected to begin in 2010.

Region celebrates landing of Toyota plant

■ **The Japanese automaker will create some 2,000 jobs with its 15th North American plant.**

BY DENNIS SEID
Daily Journal

TUPELO – Half a world away in Tokyo, while most of Northeast Mississippi was still asleep late Monday, the board of directors of Toyota Motor Corp. officially gave its final stamp of approval for a project that likely will forever change the landscape of the region.

Then all eyes turned to Tupelo, where on Tuesday morning federal, state and local leaders, joined by Toyota officials, officially announced that the company was building a $1.3 billion vehicle assembly plant at the Wellspring Project megasite near Blue Springs, 10 miles northwest of Tupelo.

Production is expected to begin in 2010 on the 1,700-acre site, which was chosen over locations in Arkansas and Tennessee.

Toyota made its decision Sunday, but news had leaked Monday that the deal was done. Officials, however, remained tight-lipped until Tuesday's event at the Tupelo High School Performing Arts Center, where the 1,500 people packed into the auditorium erupted in applause and cheers and delivered at least a dozen standing ovations in an atmosphere of festive celebration.

With broadcasts over the Web and across the world, officials sang the praises of the area, citing the cooperation, the work ethic and even the loyalty of the thousands of people who will be involved with the massive project. It will be Toyota's 15th North American manufacturing plant and its eighth assembly plant.

"We in Mississippi and especially North Mississippi are excited to have been chosen by Toyota as its partner," Gov. Haley Barbour said. "Toyota is the world's premier auto manufacturer, and our state will be the best partner Toyota has ever had."

The plant, which will build Highlander sports utility vehicles, will employ some 2,000 workers by the time production starts. Another 2,000 construction jobs will be created to build the facility, and several thousand related jobs are expected.

The $1.3 billion investment by Toyota doesn't include the state incentive package worth about $326 million, including $30 million to suppliers – less than the $363 million package offered to Nissan seven years ago. Legislators could begin work as early as Friday on approving the package.

Seiichi Sudo, right, president and COO of Toyota Motor Engineering and Manufacturing North America sports Elvis glasses Tuesday after Toyota announced that the Wellspring industrial site near Tupelo will house a new Toyota plant.

AUTOMAKER-STATE PARTNERSHIP HELPED TO CEMENT DECISION

■ **The company kept its eyes on the state after passing it up a few years ago.**

BY DENNIS SEID
Daily Journal

TUPELO – It is a Japanese concept, keiretsu, that might apply to how Toyota and Mississippi became partners.

The Japanese automaker is building a $1.3 billion vehicle assembly plant that will employ some 2,000 workers and create thousands of spinoff jobs. Company officials said they could have gone anywhere, but ultimately picked the Wellspring Project megasite not because of money, but because of the area's people.

And most important was how well everyone worked together to bring the project to fruition.

In many ways, Toyota found that working with state and local officials was much like keiretsu, a form of corporate structure where companies form a close-knit bond, working together to achieve success for all.

The system, based on close partnerships between government and businesses, links manufacturers, suppliers, distributors and a host of others.

And while there is no such thing as American keiretsu – or Mississippi keiretsu for that matter – it was clear that forging relationships was critical as Toyota worked with state and local officials.

Company representatives made sev-

Turn to **PARTNERS** on **Page 4A**

More inside on the continuing coverage of Toyota's planned facility at Wellspring

PAGE 4A

■ Legislators expect a special session to begin on Friday to take over the incentives package for the automaker.

■ Regional cooperation in the deal ensures that the wealth will be spread.

■ The Highlander is Toyota's top SUV. **4A**

PAGE 5A

■ Schools across Northeast Mississippi get a $50 million surprise from the automaker.

■ Think you want to work there. Be patient, and get in line.

PAGE 7A

■ What is higher education's role?

■ Whether it's ready or not, NE Miss. is in for changes after the announcement. **Back page**

Chapter Twenty-Six

CDF and Toyota

Over the following months, I frequently interacted with the men from the Georgetown plant about their specific needs for security. The "Toyota Way" has opened factories all over the world and has had to deal with the safety of the employees, the community, and others in a variety of settings. But there was one thing I learned very quickly.

Creating and implementing security services for a large factory with 3,000 employees is not the same as policing. I've known lots of cops who have felt they could moonlight with a security job around an industrial site, but I'm here to tell you: it ain't the same.

However, both of these cultures have the same core need: you must know your community. Landscape and culture. People and places.

You've got to know that stuff before you can have an effective security system.

David Rumbarger saw to it that I was that point person for those folks from Georgetown as they worked to set up the system here. I knew the landscape, and I also knew the culture. I was a part of that culture by birth and because of my SWAT and SOG assignments.

Those teams met with the citizens. We were their boots on the ground as they worked to clean up their neighborhoods. We knew them by name, whether the lowest of the economic classes in our town or the highest of the administrators and business people. I knew them all.

The challenges of Toyota security included not only those things you might imagine, like stolen hubcaps, but also issues like how to protect the executives who arrived for important ceremonies. We needed to figure out where those folks would be safe, what routes were secure, how and where to evacuate them in case of a threatening event, how to protect the ordinary workers who might be in the same space, and where folks would hide if they couldn't evacuate.

Furthermore, we had to identify all the high spots where a sniper might hide so our guys could get higher or be able to have a clear sight of that high spot. There was lots to think about.

Suppose a governor came to town to cut a ribbon on the Toyota factory. Lots of Toyota folks would be there, too. Everything had to be mapped out before the safety of those dignitaries could be assured. Of course, these VIPs would have their security staff with them, and we would have to coordinate with them, too.

It was not like driving a squad car with a computer at your side.

David saw to it that I was the point man for security. And before long, Toyota came sniffing around my door and asking questions about my background.

A little more than a year after I started working at CDF, my contact, Jeff, told me Toyota would be posting a security director position to oversee all the aspects of the safety of the Blue Springs Plant. He asked if I was interested in applying.

I knew he was probably behind their asking me to put in an application. He had plagued me with the same questions that the Toyota guys had asked me the first time I met them. But every time I would give all the same answers and all from my heart.

Often when I would go down to dinner with these guys, they would ask about the investigation that had led to my dismissal from the force. Then they would apologize for the treatment I had received. I don't know why because it certainly wasn't their fault, but they did. Every time.

They would say, "We like you." "You have a lot to offer." "We're glad you are here for us."

I had never even thought of leaving CDF. The thing I loved most about working there was the level of trust. Everyone there trusted everyone else. It was a form of respect each person had for the other. They wouldn't be there if they could not do the job and do it well and without being told what to do. We were all capable adults and carried out our tasks.

I loved the place.

But I decided to apply for the Toyota position nonetheless. It was an international organization, and if they hired me, it would be one more step to regaining my self-esteem, to restoring my reputation in the community, and to proving to myself that I was okay. Maybe I would be "legitimate" again.

I filled in the application and sent it off, and a few weeks later, they contacted me about the second stage of the process. I followed through, but not with any particular enthusiasm. I had a job I loved, and it would take a lot to make me change employers.

But the hiring process moved forward, and I got another call. They had narrowed the thirty or so applications down to three, and I was one of them.

Would I come up to Georgetown for the final "in-person" interview?

Well, what did I have to lose?

They made the arrangements, and I flew off to Kentucky. I had to ask myself, *What am I doing here?* The answer, of course, was, *Just seein' what it is all about.*

One thing sticks in my mind: I had forgotten to take into consideration that Kentucky is north of Tupelo. And it was a lot colder than when I left home. I had neglected to bring a winter coat with me. Man, were my hands and feet cold!

Fortunately, I had a warm hotel room.

The next morning, I got up and got dressed in my best black pinstriped suit. I tied my shiny black shoes and silently thanked Cliff again for showing me how to polish them.

At the Toyota plant, I was shown into the large lobby area. There were two other people there – clearly my competitors. One was a white woman who I understood was employed by Toyota. The other was a white man who more than likely was also a former officer. He and I eyed each other the way only cops can. That technique was called "breaking him down," and we both knew how to do it.

We had many seats to choose from in that room, but he and I both selected ones that put our backs to the walls. It was for our own protection. You learn that early on in law enforcement.

You want everything in front of you.

I sat there with my feet and hands feeling like I just took them out of the freezer, thinking all the time. Evaluating the opposition. Reviewing my own strengths. I was still not sure I wanted the job, but during the application process I had arrived at the conclusion that I could handle it. I kept remembering the staff from Georgetown telling me, "You are perfect for our point man in this area."

The other guy went first into the interview room where our fates would be decided. It took about thirty minutes before the administrative assistant called for the woman to go in next.

That meant I was last.

That was ok. I had a lot of time to ponder my strengths and my challenges. I had been in lots of these interview situations – not as the candidate, but rather as the "hirer". I knew what they were looking for and how to give them what they wanted. As my mind ran through all sorts of ideas, I knew I had to respect the Japanese culture that was built into this company. Some of the people who would be interviewing me that day were Japanese, and I had learned at CDF that learning about and respecting someone's cultural heritage is an important step in building a connection with them.

After another thirty minutes, it was my turn. I stood on my icy feet in my shiny shoes, straightened my tie, and strode off to the interview room. I had this under control. I'd been in court, for Pete's sake. I had stood in front of the judge who could have sent me to jail! After what I had been through in the past year and half, this was a piece of cake.

Walking into the room, I was met with four people at a table on a raised dais: two white males, one white female and one Asian (I assume he was Japanese) male. In addition, there was another white woman in the corner.

I could only guess at her purpose there. She did watch me like a hawk, but she never said a word.

Across from those people was an empty chair and a table with a pad and pen.

Now I had two choices: go in and sit down or walk up to the group.

I chose the latter. I walked up to their table with confidence and stood respectfully in front of their group, waiting for them to tell me what to do. I did not reach out to shake hands – that would be "American," and I had been learning about the "Toyota Way," which is definitely Asian. They nodded and indicated I could sit down.

I had to be respectful, leave distance between them and me, let them initiate the conversation, and allow them to direct me. I kept good eye contact with each of them in order to create a sense of trust. Different cultures have different values. I was American, and the company was Japanese. There was lots to learn.

One of the white men was my new buddy Jeff, who had urged me to apply. However, at that moment, he had his game face on. There was no friendship in these exchanges. The job was up for the best candidate, and I had to prove I was the guy for the job.

They asked the predictable questions: Why do you think you are particularly qualified to be a Toyota employee? What would you want to see happen between the company and the community? And on and on. Typical interview questions that I myself had asked many times before.

I was eternally grateful for the courses I had taken both at the police academy and especially at the FBI academy. That was where I had learned about communication and how to do it well.

When that phase of the interview ended, the other candidates and I were led off to separate rooms and given a big blank piece of paper and a pen. We were given a scenario, and our assignment was to describe how we would handle such a situation.

"You are the head of security affairs at Toyota, a plant which employs 2,000 to 3,000 persons. The plant has just received a bomb threat. Tell us what you would do."

We were given about another thirty minutes to complete our scenarios before we presented them to the interview board, and mercifully, I was last again.

I don't know what the others did with the circumstances, but I felt very at home.

I began to think about my answer. I know I'd had this kind of experience before.

First, I would have to take into consideration that, in addition to a bomb threat, there might be a sniper hiding in a high place in order to attack all the frightened people who would be vacating the building. So, where were the high places? Where could we put defenses to take out the sniper? How would we evacuate all those loyal employees so they can go home to their families at the end of this day?

And, what if we had the governor touring the building? And the president of Toyota International there to meet and greet the governor? Where was a "safe place" within the building for those "special" people to go? How could they be protected on their way to that location? Or, better yet, was there a safe way to leave the building where they could meet up with the emergency responders?

Where could emergency responders – fire, police, medical personnel – park to be most effective in such a situation? How, where, and when would we brief the CEOs about their evacuation routes, etc.?

I'd had actual experience in that situation. I had had to protect B.B. King, Jesse Jackson, and Smokey Robinson during my work with the TPD. (I had accompanied them from Tunica to Birmingham and on to Atlanta. I even have a "thank you" note from him for my work.) This was not a new situation for me.

Law enforcement officers are forced to make these decisions quickly, but security in this industry can have plans in place in order to protect not only their people, but also to protect the manufacturing process. We wouldn't have to make those decisions instantly. We would study and plan and experiment with ideas until we got the one that worked best.

I finished my presentation, and the interview was over. We said our farewells, and I headed for the airport.

About three days later, on a Sunday, I was sitting in my leather recliner chair in the den at home. I could see out the windows, and I sat near the fireplace.

That was my comfort place. I had taken root there and it was home.

I was watching TV when the phone rang. On the other end of the line, Jeff – my Toyota buddy – asked, "You ready to come to work for Toyota?"

I was stunned. I had never dreamed I would get it.

"Will I have any time to think about it?"

"Sure," he replied. "How about a week from tomorrow we make a decision?"

That sounded good to me, so we agreed. I had seven days to make my choice.

I had always wanted to be a cop. That route had been snatched from me in 2006, but CDF had been right there, as were the leaders in Tupelo, to take care of me and nurture me in another field.

A field, by the way, that I really loved.

I went to work the next day and talked to David. "What am I going to do?" I asked him.

"That's pretty awesome, Robert. Toyota wants you and we want you. Two major organizations. Not a bad spot to be in."

Why would I even consider changing from CDF to Toyota? I didn't have a strong reason, because I was truly happy there. I was working within the community in an environment that I loved. One full of trust that we could all do our jobs and do them well.

But, my reputation had been "sullied," and I saw this as an opportunity to save face.

I would be in a highly paid position with an international company, communicating with company leaders from all over the country – California and Detroit, as well as Kentucky. I would be part of the planning for new sites and reviewing processes if problems arose.

I would not exactly be with law enforcement, but I would still be connected to the field.

But most of all, I would be able to hold my head up high because *outsiders* would be recognizing my worth.

So on that next Monday, I accepted the offer from Toyota to be their director of security services. Oh, and they upped my salary even more than CDF had. That was good, too.

I even surprised myself with that decision, but I did it.

Leaving CDF was hard, even though I had not been there for a long time. David had been a very special mentor to me. He had taught me to have faith in the folks around me and to trust their skills and talents, among many other things. He was my personification of the word "integrity".

David Rumbarger was my model of a good leader.

Chapter Twenty-Seven

Toyota Security

I began my tenure at Toyota by working in a building owned by CDF – the IDEA center. It was a place where folks with new ideas for a business could get cheap rent for a year or two in order to get their enterprise off the ground. I missed the folks in the old post office, but I like the people in the IDEA Center. Wayne Averett was also a CDF worker, and we already knew each other, so it wasn't like I was going to a really new place. But this wasn't CDF – it was Toyota.

Our offices were on the second floor of the IDEA Center, so my first day I trudged up the steps to begin my new job.

What am I doing here? I thought as I climbed each step. *I'm supposed to be a policeman!*

Well, that was before. This was the new chapter of my life. Post-TPD, post-CDF – now I was a Toyota guy.

I had helped Toyota get settled at the IDEA Center when I was the liaison between them and CDF so I knew where I was going. I had helped them lay out the plan for the office that now opened up before me.

It was familiar. There were temporary walls between the cubicles where folks like me did our work. On the walls were hundreds of plans, graphs, and other drawings of where things would go once the plant was constructed. Along the walls, people sat in their offices, quietly working on their particular area of expertise. A few of the cubicles had doors, but most did not. Those were the offices of the executives, where you could have a "private" meeting if necessary. Otherwise, even the big bosses had the same size offices that the rest of us did. That was the Toyota way, too.

I was reminded of my first day at CDF. Everyone was so serious. I might try to crack a joke, and the people I was chatting with would seem unsure of what they should do. "Should we laugh? Was he joking or was he being sarcastic?" In both places, it took a bit before my coworkers knew me well enough to recognize an attempt at humor.

I got settled in and began building relationships with the Toyota folks. There were people involved with building maintenance, folks designing office spaces, and men who were planning where the presses would go. They were all talking about things like where the trucks would come and go from and how long they would be there before they were fully loaded and ready to depart. And the head of the entire operation was there, in his cubicle that looked like all the rest. They were creating a synchronized movement – almost like a ballet has to be choreographed – to get things done the Toyota Way.

My first task was to learn how Toyota worked and where I fit in. They didn't want my physical labor – they wanted my brain.

Now, I was not used to that. I had been used to sitting for a short bit before getting up, getting into the car, and driving around. Keeping my eyes and ears open to see what might be happening. Sitting at a desk was not really my cup of tea.

Toyota takes their ideas from the workers wherever they are, including the guys on the lines. Then they research that suggestion and decide whether to go with it or not. What works in Georgetown might work in Tupelo – or it might not. I had to figure that out.

I also had to keep up relationships with the emergency responders. I had to work with the hospital, fire department, and police to see exactly what kind of resources they might need and where they were located. We had to solve problems like how medical specialists could get in and out of any place on the property to give aid.

In addition, I had to review and evaluate the security companies that Toyota hired to do the actual work on the ground. They would hire two or three different companies to provide personnel to guard the entrances and so on. Whereas I would usually look at hiring each individual person I needed, these companies were under contract and would do their own hiring. I had to make sure the security companies were always doing what they were supposed to do.

I had to hunker down and learn the Toyota way of doing things. My friend Dr. Grisham once remarked on a dinner he attended in the early days of Toyota in Tupelo. It was a banquet where he was seated next to a top executive with the company.

"We are not an easy company to work for," the executive said to Dr. Grisham. "We know how we want things done, and we expect you to do it that way. If we order parts from you, we want it put in a specific place in a particular manner."

And he was right. They research things thoroughly, so when they arrive at a way of getting things done, it has been through a good deal of thinking.

I had to learn the Toyota way of thinking.

In addition to my new responsibilities, I still filled the liaison role for the community and the company, even after I came on board with them. Toyota still knew me as the guy with the local connections.

Their Japanese workers were moving to Tupelo, Asian culture and all. I was slowly getting familiar with the values they had that differed from ours, but it would be foolish to suggest I had them all mastered.

One time, I got a call before I left for work. One of the Japanese leaders' homes had been broken into. I drove straight over to see how I could help.

This was a nice neighborhood, with homes ranging from $280,000 to $300,000 (in 2008 prices, that is). The home in question was brick, which I always thought of as being better. I pulled in the driveway and walked up to the front door.

I rang the doorbell, and the Japanese executive opened the door.

When I entered, he bowed to me, and I bowed back. Looking around, I could tell immediately I was in one of the most orderly places I had ever seen. Everything was in its proper place. Nothing looked as though it was casually placed – no recently read newspapers, no half-finished cups of coffee.

No. Everything was in its place.

He knew enough English to tell me what had happened, and I told him we would get with the police and get it taken care of.

We needed to document the event and the area.

This man knew where *everything* in his home was placed. These things were important to him, and he was able to give good, detailed information.

We made our way to his bedroom where he opened the closet door.

Shoe stores aren't that organized.

All the footwear was placed in a very orderly manner. He told me what size shoes he had; he knew the height of the heels on each of them, whether short or taller. Some shirts were gone, and some vests were, too. There was a place for everything, and he knew when everything was in its place. And when it was not in its place!

I called the sheriff – the same man who had wanted me out of my TPD job.

He was most cooperative because he knew the importance of dealing with these people. He had been at the meetings.

He assigned an officer to come out to the home and take the information from the Toyota executive. The officer who responded had been one of those assigned to go to Jim Waide's office to arrest me. But there was nothing of that in our exchanges that day. He knew he had to deal with me and, like the sheriff, was most cooperative.

The officers took the report, and I told the homeowner that the sheriff's office was in complete control and would take care of everything.

That was the end of that.

They thought they needed my brain, but they also needed my understanding of the local culture. And I knew how to merge our culture successfully with the culture of Toyota.

So, for the next several months I sat at my desk most of the time, dealing with ideas, plans, and projects. I was enrolled in a leadership course at Toyota, which was most valuable.

But all the time, I kept thinking, *I'm supposed to be a policeman. I really wanted to be a policeman.* I had somehow thought that this position would help bridge the gap between me and my former career, but it didn't.

I learned so much there, just like at CDF. I learned that there are places to work where people don't judge you on the color of your skin, but on the value of your knowledge and your ability to learn. People took me at face value. I had been so deceived before. I thought the folks who worked with me would support me through anything, but some of them didn't.

CDF and Toyota showed me there are plenty of businesses where the people out there will support you.

What I learned most from Toyota was the focus of getting the job done. We worked together to reach our goal of getting cars out of the plant and into their new owner's hands efficiently, effectively, and cleanly.

As with CDF, I learned new dimensions of leadership from Toyota, too. I became familiar with the elements that make up a good leader, from watching an extraordinary one like David Rumbarger to learning the basic principles at Toyota.

Those two experiences were incredibly valuable to me, and I would simply not be the man I am without those two jobs.

But I still wanted to go back to being a policeman.

So, when Jack Reed, Jr., the son of the man who had given me advice on my ideas at CDF, called and told me he was going to run for mayor of Tupelo, I thought, *Maybe the town will get right now.*

Jack had been called to a meeting with about five or six of his friends and leaders in town. They met for lunch and encouraged him to run for mayor, since the incumbent was not going to run for another term. He told me that he had been flattered, but he had respectfully declined. He had said in no uncertain terms that he was content doing what he was doing – running the Reed's Department stores and volunteering, rather than taking pay for working for the good of the community.

He had recently served as the president of CDF, so he thought that was why they had spoken to him. But Jack told me he had been happy saying, "Thanks, but no thanks." He had gone home and told his wife, Lisa, about the meeting, and they had both agreed. It was quite an honor, but the answer was "no".

Sometime later, Jack told me, the same group had called again and asked if both he *and* Lisa would meet them for lunch.

So, they had, and the conversation had centered on the need for improvement in the town. Now, remember, Tupelo was a true leader in the state of Mississippi and had received many awards citing our extraordinary growth and progress.

A deal had been struck: Lisa and Jack didn't feel comfortable asking others for money, so the group had agreed to do the fundraising for the election campaign.

The couple went home and talked with their kids and with Jack Reed, Sr., Jack's dad, about the pros and cons of running for office. Jack Reed, Sr., had run for governor back in the late 1980s, and Jack, Jr., and Lisa well remembered that experience.

Jack, Jr., said one person had said something that made a difference to him: Monte Fox, an associate of Billy Crews at the *Daily Journal.* Monte commented, "You'd be able to extend your circle of influence."

That had done it. Jack was running for mayor. He talked to me about it because I was a good representative of the black community in town. He wanted to know what I thought.

I was thrilled to death. Jack as mayor would be a leap forward toward getting the races to trust each other again. I jumped on his band wagon.

He won.

It was a very positive move in the right direction.

Among the first things he did was to encourage the former chief of police to retire. Then, he appointed Tony Carleton as chief of police.

Jack Reed, Jr., and Robert at Robert's Drum Major Award ceremony, 2024

Chapter Twenty-Eight

Changing the Guard

Toyota had given me back my sense of self-worth. I was an administrator in one of the leading international corporations in the world, and I was making a lot more money than I had been in law enforcement.

While Jack Reed, Jr., and I spoke often to each other, it was just to "catch up". He had supported my cause all during the down days, and we had had a strong friendship over the past four years.

Both before and immediately after his election, he never spoke to me about coming back to work at the TPD. It was never part of our conversations.

I continued to work at Toyota for the next two years. In fact, as close as I was to Jack, I wasn't even able to attend his inaugural ceremony. He moved into office smoothly and got busy on his agenda: making Tupelo a better place for all its citizens.

He put a new, progressive chief in the open job after the old chief left. Chief Tony Carleton moved into the office formerly held by the chief that had supported my being charged with felonies and being fired.

I was glad to see that man retire. Interestingly, he was hired by the sheriff after leaving the chief's role, but he was not able to physically handle the job of bailiff in the county court. Within a short time, he fully retired to his home. He has been in poor health ever since.

There were folks at city hall who wanted to see me back at TPD. I had become a metaphor for justice among some folks – I represented mistreatment of the black people.

As Toyota's informal liaison between the races in Tupelo, I was a member of the Mission Mississippi group. Their focus is on working on racial relations, emphasizing respect between the races and I believed deeply in their work. After one meeting, Jack Reed, Sr., waved me over.

"Come with me to the car. I need to talk to you," he said. I agreed, and we walked out to the curb, where his old blue Buick station wagon with the wood panels along the side was parked. He got in on the driver's side, and I slid in on my side.

He didn't even look at me at first – in fact, he was gazing out of the front windshield when he said in his very unique Southern accent, "Rawbuht, it's time you came back." I swear, he looked almost like the Godfather issuing an edict. He was a very powerful man in the state, and he was very serious. And he still didn't look at me when he repeated, "I think it's time for you to come back."

It had been three years since I had been separated from the force.

I didn't know how to respond. I knew a part of me wanted to go back to the police force. In my heart, I was still a cop. But a part of me also wanted to go back for revenge! I knew that the idea was tugging at me, but I didn't say that.

What I said was, "I appreciate your confidence in me, and I will do the best I can to not let you down." I knew I would never let people like him and his son down if I could possibly avoid it.

One day in 2010, I was leaving the barber shop when my phone rang.

Chief Carleton was on the other end of the line. "You ready?"

"Ready for what?" I asked.

"Ready to put the uniform on and go to work," he said.

"You are kidding me!"

"No, I'm not. I want you back as my deputy chief. That position has been open for too long now."

Talk about a bittersweet moment. I wanted it. I had never stopped being a cop. I would listen to the news, watch the tv reports, and mentally argue or agree with the actions taken by the department or specific officers.

One side of me said, *Your law enforcement career is over.* I was out of the loop of being a cop. And then there was my family. How would this affect them? What would they say? They were four years older now. I knew I had to get their opinions: Melissa, Marissa, Brandon, and Terrell.

The other side said, *Get back in and show them!*

I asked if I could have a couple of days to think about it.

Of course, he said yes.

At home, Melissa gave me her usual support. "Whatever you decide is okay with me. It's your decision to make."

You know, there's something about being a career cop. I had seen it in myself, and I had seen it in others. Most of us cannot deal with being off the streets. Even when you think you want to retire, you get out of the uniform and put your gun up, and bingo…you still want to be back on the force.

Well, that's the way it was with me. I still wanted to be a cop. I was born to be on the streets. I had twenty years of being in law enforcement, ranging from the dispatcher to the deputy chief.

I am a cop at heart

So, I told the family of my decision, and then called Chief Carleton.

"Chief", I said when he answered the phone. "I'm going to come back. Thanks to you for the offer."

Then, I dialed Jeff's number at Toyota.

"Jeff," I began, "maybe I'm nuts, but I'm going to go back to the Tupelo Police Department as Deputy Chief. I believe at heart I am a cop. But you folks at Toyota have been great to me."

"You're right! You must be nuts!" was Jeff's immediate response. "You're a sucker for punishment. But, if it is what you want, Toyota will respect it."

Toyota was absolutely wonderful about my decision. They said I would always have a place there, but they understood. In the early days of their being here in Tupelo, they had educated themselves about my situation, and I'm sure they were wondering why in the name of heaven I would go back there.

But all they emphasized to me was, "You have a home here any time."

I gave them a little less than two weeks notice, but I did stay in contact with them in case any issues came up that I could help with.

I was eternally grateful for their support.

The chief and I discussed the particulars of me coming back to work. He had checked with the state regulations, and there was no real need for recertification.

I would have to qualify at the shooting range with at least a 75 score and take a few courses at the training center or the academy to freshen up my knowledge of the laws that had been passed in the years between 2006 and 2010.

The Board of Standards in Policing would have to approve my recertification, but they handled those requests all the time. There were rarely complications.

I was assured that there would not need to be any formal process around my recertification. Once I qualified at the shooting range and passed my courses, that was it. My background in terms of my experience was impeccable. I was set.

Just to be sure, I even called the guy at the state level about my recertification. I got the same answer: qualify at the range and take a few courses. That was all.

I was set to go.

Chapter Twenty-Nine

Back In the Saddle

Chief Carleton was very supportive of my moving into the position. He made sure I had the key to my squad car in advance of my first day, and Anthony Hill drove me to the station prior to my first day on the job. Chief Carleton got my uniforms and brought them out to the house. I was all ready to go to work on March 29, 2010.

The night before, I slept not one wink. It was one of those times where you keep saying to yourself, *Did I do the right thing? What have I done?*

So, around 5:25 am, I got out of bed, showered, and dressed in my uniform.

It felt good to be back in those dark blues, with the holster at my side and my Glock in it. This wasn't the Glock 10-38 with seventeen bullets that the patrolmen carry – no, sir. Theirs were bigger and had more firepower.

I had the administrator's version. It was a compact Glock for officials, but there was one in the chamber and ten in the clip.

I got in the car – not a brand-new Crown Victoria, but a fairly new one with all the bells and whistles, plus an AR15 and a rifle.

I drove down toward town about 7:45 a.m., taking a different route than usual. I had always liked to drive down Green Street because it was a rough part of town, and I liked to know what might be going on. I still had the sense of patrolling.

This time I took the bypass by McCullough. I had not been there since the incident in 2006, but when I came up on the area, I didn't take the route that would go past the scene. I drove on so I didn't have to pass that place. I didn't go past Hardee's, either. Even though I loved their bacon, egg, and cheese biscuit, I would not go there. Call it superstition, call it whatever. I just couldn't go back there.

Even though so much time has passed since the event I still don't pass those places unless I absolutely have to.

The Tuesday after the incident, Allan went in to confess. He admitted he had left the scene of the accident, he was found guilty, and though his sentence was seven years, he served three and was released. He has since married and has beautiful children and a supervisory job in a factory. His wife works in a bank, and his life is quite good.

I still think I did the right thing by not leaving him in the hands of those two policemen who had a record of being abusive to black men.

I drove on and parked in the police station parking lot.

I walked through the main office, where the dispatcher, administrative assistants, jailer, and others had their desks, and I was greeted in general by smiles and warm welcomes. Of course, not everyone saw me the same way. The officers who had been involved in the situation in 2006 ignored me – in fact, they looked as though they had seen a ghost.

Interestingly, they were ignoring the very person who would be giving them orders. That takes guts. I believed they already knew they had a plan to get rid of me again.

They had a plan, and they had support in high places. The two or three city council members who had wanted me off the force in the beginning were still on the board. The sheriff was the same man. The district attorney was the same person. And even though the chief was gone, the same people who mistreated blacks were still on the force.

But I knew I had the support of the chief because he had been on SWAT and SOG with me. When he was the "newbie" on the force and was the brunt of lots of hazing, I told him that I had his back. He didn't even have to tell me that on that first day.

I knew he had my back.

It was a good thing, too, because the white "intimidators" who had been hovering across the street from my house during the days of the suspension were back. They would pull up in that parking lot and just sit there – during the day, at night. Not on a regular schedule, but just any time. I couldn't predict when they would be there.

March 16, 2010, an article appeared in the *Journal* with the headline "Robert Hall returns to the Tupelo Police Department." That article began, "Former Deputy Police Chief Robert Hall will be in the department March 29 as second in command of the 127-member force."

Following that was an interesting restatement of the facts of the case. For instance, it said, "...On May 28, 2006, Hall set free 20-year old Allan Denton after he been arrested for running over a teenage bicyclist and leaving the scene." That was a misrepresentation that spoke volumes. I didn't "set him free" – he was released on his own recognizance which means he must report at a given time to the police department.

It seemed lines were already being drawn.

Chapter Thirty

A Town Divided – Again

My return divided the town again. Council member Nettie Davis thought my hiring was a wise move to try and bridge the gap between the races. Others were not so supportive.

The *Daily Journal* reported that Councilman Markel Whittington called the move a mistake. "As I have shared with the mayor and chief, I am afraid this will be a huge distraction for the city, and it will *question the credibility of the police department.* Though I strongly disagree with this hire, I will continue to support the police department and all the other city departments."

On March 25, there was an editorial in the *Journal* that said my hiring had "stirred substantial but measured controversy at Tuesday night's City Council meeting." The article emphasized that I had pleaded guilty to the misdemeanor charge after what they termed "mishandling a never proven DUI hit-and-run case."

The article went on, "Concerns and objections were freely expressed by three council members and one citizen.... Mayor Jack Reed, Jr. stood behind Chief of Police Tony Carleton's decision to hire Hall.

"Responsibility clearly falls onto Carleton and Hall to justify Hall's new hiring with the stellar performance of the same quality and consistency that marked Hall's first Tupelo Police Department work prior to the incident that led to his departure....Carleton made the hiring decision because he has known Hall for a long time, worked with him, and has seen his work as a police officer and administrator. Carleton is new to the chief's position, but he is an experienced law enforcement leader, and his judgment should be given a chance to prove itself."

Things were a bit quieter after the paper urged folks to give me and Carleton's decision to hire me a chance. I decided to go out to the shooting range and test my skills. I knew I wasn't in top-notch shape, but I wanted to try to get into that sharp place where I had been in June of 2006 when all this had begun.

I drove out to the shooting range and went through the tests. A 75 score is passing and means that a person would be recertified to carry a gun. But I wasn't satisfied with a 75. I wanted to be close to perfect. Seventy-five was a failure to me.

Well, my first testing saw me get an 88 score. Way above what I would need to be recertified. Not good enough for me, though. I didn't want to have a less-than-perfect ability when I was aiming at a suspect or trying to avoid innocent bystanders. I needed a perfect score. *I'll come back and work on that later on*, I thought.

Back in the office, there were still two different attitudes about my return: some who were for me and others who were against me.

The next time I appeared in the paper was in June. On the fifth day of that month, another article by Mr. Elkins appeared with the headline "Chief: Hall recertification not needed."

That article stated that I didn't have arrest powers, but that I could work as an administrator. And the chief indicated that that was where I was needed. "He's in an administrative position, and his job is to focus on improving policies and procedures and to help the department to connect with the community so we all can have a good working relationship."

The Board of Standards, which would make the decision about my recertification, was led by the same sheriff who had been involved in firing me in the first place.

He was quoted in the *Daily Journal* as saying, "We were told there had been no request for his certificate. We don't know what the delay has been in applying for it."

Mayor Reed said in the article that he was satisfied with the job I was doing at the time and that I had added a lot of leadership and energy to the department. "I think he has already proven his value to the city and department since he was brought on."

But other forces were at work. In late June, an anonymous letter appeared in the mailboxes of many of Tupelo's citizens.

It was a two-paged, unsigned letter, which described the May 2006 incident. It also attacked my return in 2010. Finally, it urged its readers to call the mayor or the police chief and complain.

The handwriting on the wall was clear to me. I had made a mistake. In fact, I often describe my decision to leave Toyota as both the best and the worst decision of my life.

The problems were starting up again. I would stay and fight, but my heart wasn't in it. I wasn't going to win, no matter how much I wanted to. The balance of power was not in my favor.

My face continued to appear in the *Journal* that summer.

On June 13, an article ran entitled, "Diversity Complaint Leveled at Sheriff: Ripples continued to spread from the rehiring of Robert Hall as Tupelo's Deputy Police Chief." The article read, "The Coalition of African-American Organizations attacked [the] Sheriff for a lack of diversity in his department and threatened to file a complaint with the Department of Justice. [He] retaliated by saying that group was harassing him. He charged they were blaming him for this role as the head of the Board of Law Enforcement Standards and Training which would have to recertify Hall."

The sheriff also claimed that Mayor Reed had "demanded" that the board recertify me. The mayor's reply was simple: "That conversation was confidential."

By August, the city council urged the police chief to recertify me. While this is a procedural thing, usually not an issue, this time it was going to be. Plain and simple. They wanted me to go before the board headed by the man who had backed my firing to begin with and see if I could become recertified.

The city council said the department's goals for the upcoming year "would not go ahead" without my recertification.

I wish I could convey all that I was thinking and what I was going through during those days.

I was trying to do my job as the deputy chief – reaching across the racial lines to try and diffuse any battle lines that might be drawn. I was creeping out in the dark of night to watch those white supremacists who parked across from my house to intimidate me and my family. I was trying to be a good father and a good husband, as well as continue to be active in my church and in the community. It was a nightmare.

Then the Klan decided to officially get into it. They wanted to march against my hiring. In fact, the quote I heard was that they knew they had to "come down here and take care of some uppity black cop." They decided to hold a march, but they knew they would not get a permit if they applied to the city.

So, they applied to the county, where people like the Lee County sheriff (the same man who held the power to decide if I would be recertified) would be in charge of accepting or rejecting the application for a parade. They applied to hold a meeting on the county courthouse grounds.

And it was approved.

I got a call from the head of the NAACP. "Robert Hall?" he said.

I answered, "Yes."

"I've just gotten a call from Reverend Al Sharpton's office. You remember he's that outstanding civil rights supporter. He's appeared around the nation anytime there has been such issues as are going on in Tupelo."

He continued, "Al Sharpton's office wanted to know if they should come on down to draw attention to the story. You know when he appears, the national media descends on the area and publicizes the relevant issues. What do you think? Shall we set a date for him to come and speak on your behalf?"

My response was easy. "When someone like Al Sharpton comes to town, it does hit the media – newspaper and TV reporters show up all over the place. So do big vans with the local TV call letters on the sides, as well as major TV affiliates – CBS, NBC, ABC, Fox, and all the rest. Tents covering the cameras appear all over the sidewalks around the courthouse, and lots of media personnel are shoving microphones in ordinary citizens' faces, as well as chasing after all the key 'players' in the case. They are interviewing them, and they are always glad to talk.

"But you know what?" I went on. "When they leave, the locals are still in their own town and must deal with the aftermath. I don't want that to happen to me or to Tupelo."

I graciously told him, "Once the Sharpton folks leave, I still have to live here. It's not worth the effort."

And I'm glad I did.

As of late August, the council wanted to treat me like a trainee unless and until I got recertified. It would mean a nearly $30,000 drop in salary. Councilwoman Nettie Davis argued that they "might be igniting another racial uproar."

On August 30, my request for recertification was denied. When we asked for the reasons for denial, it was that the city had lost confidence in me as a policeman. How do you measure that?

Do you think they asked any black folks if they had confidence in me?

Chapter Thirty-One

2010 Recertification Appeal

As in so many of the litigation situations in America, there is an appeal process. So, even I had the right to appeal my denial.

And I did. Jim Waide set the stage for this next argument. The date was set for November 4, 2010, in Pearl, Mississippi – that town where I had spent so many happy weeks learning to be a good cop.

Cliff, Jim, and I prepared for that appeal hearing.

Jim Waide volunteered his time to defend me, and my old friend Cliff was still on my side. He knew me and would stand up for me. I could never understand the folks who knew me and were against me.

Jack Reed, Jr., continued to call just to check on me, and when the calendar page read November 3, I packed a small bag for the overnight in Pearl.

The day was coming.

Chief Tony Carleton and I drove down the evening before and checked into the hotel where we were all staying overnight. As Tony walked with me to my room, he said "Sleep well – although I bet you won't really get much sleep tonight."

Was he ever right. My mind was going ninety-to-nothing all night. I reran how I had gotten here – what had happened to me in between May 28, 2006, and today. It was nothing but toss, turn, toss, turn all night long.

Since the meeting was scheduled for 8:30 am, I was up, showered, and dressed by 7. I went down to the lobby to catch breakfast, and there were my friends, waiting for me.

Jack Reed, Jr.; Cliff Hardy; Jim Waide; and Tony Carleton were all part of my team. They were there to support me in this effort, one more time, to get me back on the force.

Danza Johnson, a *Journal* reporter came along, too, and it's a good thing. There were no records of that appeal, and his reports are all the hard evidence we have of what went on.

Dr. Ed Holiday, a dentist from Tupelo, came as well. Now, let me tell you, he is a rock rib Republican, not even close to my political persuasion. But there he was. He had even closed his dental offices for the day so he could be there.

And he didn't even have a dog in that hunt. He was just there for my support. He was there because he knew what was right and what was wrong.

I can tell you, knowing my friends were in the audience really made me feel good. I had a stellar team. I looked at those men who were in my corner, and I was proud. These men, all white, knew what I was made of and were not going to let this issue go without a fight.

I thought for a minute of all the innocent people, both black and white, who had been wrongfully convicted and did not have access to the quality team I had. I ached for them.

We grabbed our free breakfast, the others got something to eat, and we headed out to the Pearl Academy. That was where the hearing would be held.

As we drove onto the campus, I remembered the first time I had been there. It had been 1987 when I was heading into my new career. I could never have imagined then what an incredible journey I would have in that career – until 2006. Now I was here to defend that career.

We found the meeting room and went in. It was set up rather like a courtroom, but there were some key differences. A long table for the thirteen-member board sat in the front of the room. There was a place for anyone giving testimony to sit and lots of chairs for those curious souls who were there for the show.

We arrived well before the 8:30 am commencement time, but nothing happened. Time and time again, the board, which was meeting in a room off the main room, would send out word that they were not ready to start the hearing.

Sometime later, two DAs who I had worked closely with entered the room. Clearly, they were the reason for the delays.

From here on, I will rely on Danza's reporting of the meeting to support my memory of the appeal hearing from the newspaper. He did a good job of documenting the key statements, times, and other important points of this meeting. I have asked and asked but have been told there is no formal record of this hearing, so I can't provide the official record of what happened.

But we do have Danza's records.

Finally, about 11 am, the testimonies started.

One witness, a district attorney, testified, "Giving Hall back his certification could open other cases. Never would I have thought Hall would be hired back. This is not the kind of officer you want out there handling cases." [1]

I also remember him claiming that I had formulated a plan to get Denton off, when later in the testimony someone stated that I encouraged the officers to continue the investigation of the Denton incident. That DA further accused me of "flexing my muscles" to get Denton off.

The two DAs had driven down from North Mississippi to make these statements, which I knew to be lies.

What I hated was that those comments were made to people who didn't know me. The DAs both knew me and had trusted me to guard their homes when they were in danger. One of them had received threats from a murderer, and Cliff and I guarded his home all night while my family, who had also been threatened, were left without anyone to protect them. I had worked with these men on many cases where we successfully brought criminals to justice.

I still ask the question, "Why would they do this to me?"

---

1 *Northeast Mississippi Daily Journal*, November 4, 2010

It also seemed to me that the entire case against me hinged on the testimonies of these two district attorneys. They were the ones who had been late, and the entire trial had been held until they arrived. If these witnesses were just a part of a large pool of evidence, why hadn't we been able to start without them?

Back to the record from the *Journal* writer.

The Tupelo City Attorney, John Hill, presented letters in support of me. Those included ones from former Mayor Larry Otis, Doyce Deas, Community Development Foundation Executive Director David Rumbarger, and others. *White* community leaders in my hometown stood up for me. Hill also repeated that I had "told the officers to continue the investigation" against Allan Denton.

At 1:20 p.m. on that Thursday, "Tupelo Police Chief Tony Carleton told the Board he re-hired [me] because he noticed dissension and other inconsistencies in the department. That [I] had built a great rapport with the black community, had done a great job helping organize the department and had twenty years of exemplary service."

According to the *Daily Journal* article, after Carleton testified, Attorney Jim Waide, Mayor Jack Reed, Jr., and Cliff Hardy, would testify, and then I would go on the stand.

There is no copy that covers what Waide or Reed said, but there are some of the words of my dear friend and partner, Cliff Hardy.

At 2:22 p.m., Cliff began his testimony. The *Journal* reported, "Hardy said he believed jealousy and racial animosity by certain factions in the department led to Hall being fired. He said the firing was politically motivated.

"Hardy also said one of the reasons Hall did what he did at the hit-and-run was because one of the officers on the scene had a reputation for mistreating blacks and had been talked to by the department.

"The county sheriff, who was chairing the meeting, then asked if every time that officer arrested a black man if it was Hall's job to turn him loose.

"Hardy said, 'That is a ridiculous statement. What brought you to that conclusion?'

"The Sheriff said that is what he understood Hardy to be saying.

"Hardy said this is not what he was saying, and he was sorry he got that out of his testimony. He added he didn't understand how the Sheriff felt that way."

At 3:24 p.m., Mayor Jack Reed, Jr., testified. Reed said the sheriff's insinuation that he forced Carleton to hire me was not true. Reed said I had helped to bring racial harmony back to the city and allowed Tupelo to be safer.

I listened to all these statements. The statements supporting me were numerous and positive, talking about my ability to bring the races together and my exemplary background and experience.

Yet those two DAs spoke with so much anger and near-hatred that I was afraid. I sensed that this was a done deal, and not one in my favor. Here sat thirteen people who didn't know me or what I was like, hearing that I could be plotting to free all black suspects. Hearing that I was "flexing" my powers as a black deputy chief.

At some point when there was a break, the lone black man on the panel got up and left. As he passed through the audience, he was heard saying, "I'm done with this." He did not come back.

A couple of weeks later, that same man was in Tupelo, and he sought me out. I'll never forget what he said.

He told me, "There was so much racism in that room, I couldn't stand it." It reminded me forcefully of the words I had heard from the black man on the grand jury when I was being charged with a felony.

At 3:39 p.m. I began my testimony.

I told them "that (I) have always done my job, even arresting family members when necessary in the past."

They asked me why I pled guilty to the misdemeanors if I was innocent.

I answered, "At that time, I had gone from being one of the most recognizable officers in the state to having to defend my freedom. I had no source of income and a wife and three kids to take care of. I faced my word against the five other officers. I made a choice for my family to plead guilty and to stay out of jail so I could move forward with my life.

"[I] had a job offer from CDF, so [I] pleaded guilty and took the job."[2]

It was 5:05 p.m., and the testimony was done. The board went into executive session.

My heart was pounding. I felt like sweat was pouring off my head. My entire career was on exhibit, and I felt the opposition had skewed the scene to get me fired from police work forever.

The executive session of the Board of Law Enforcement Officer Standards and Training filed into the room rather somberly.

At 5:31 p.m. on November 4, 2010, the 10-1 vote was announced, and my application for recertification was denied. Had the lone black man on the board stayed to vote, there might have been one more vote in my favor.

As you might expect, Tony had made arrangements for me to leave the building through a side door so as not to have to deal with the hordes of media waiting outside for the verdict. I am grateful to Tony and my other supporters for many things, that among them.

But, even though we could appeal through the Lee County system, it would be fruitless.

My fate was sealed, and I was out of a job.

It was the end of my life as a cop.

---

2 Ibid.

Epilogue

I walked outside after boxing up my belongings.

"I will never set foot in the Tupelo Police Station again as long as I live," I vowed. "Not this station or the new one being built. "

"Never. Never. Never." I said it to myself at least twenty times.

Time marches on – poets have compared this phenomenon with the endless waves of the ocean (sometimes angry, sometimes soothing) the shifting, drifting sands of the earth, and those beautiful white puffy clouds that move from thunderous, water-filled creations in the sky into placid, feathery cirrus shapes.

They are right. Nothing stays the same. We are born, and as we grow our world expands. We become adults, marry, have children, have a career, and then we retire and continue to change. Only this time, our world begins to contract. Soon we are like children again – in a small world of our family and our hometown – hopefully.

Time moves on, and so did I.

At that moment, though, I really was in a "what next" kind of place. I was standing on the small side entry to the TPD holding a box with the meager bits and pieces of my law enforcement career in my hands. These were the personal effects of nearly twenty years on record as a cop and a six-month attempt at a return.

I loaded up my truck to drive home. I turned left out of the parking lot and onto Front Street, headed toward the corner where Elvis's mom bought his first guitar at Tupelo Hardware.

Out of a job.

My cell phone rang. We all had them in our pockets these days. It was a reminder of how much things had changed in the few short years since I had left.

"Robert Hall?" the voice asked.

"Yes," I answered.

"This is Jim Brown from Modern Woodmen of America. I'd like to meet up with you and convince you that there's a place for you in our organization. When could we meet?"

I had heard of Modern Woodmen of America, and I knew they sold insurance, but me? Sell insurance? I don't think so.

But five months later, I realized I had to do something. While my "fairy godfathers" continued to send me money to stay out of debt, I couldn't plan on that forever. I needed a job.

Jim Brown just kept calling.

And I had reached the end of my rope, so I joined the firm and learned to be an insurance salesman.

Modern Woodmen of America knew I had a wide base of people who trusted me, and they thought I could make some money with that. Once I hired on, I could see that there was a place to help folks in this industry. Besides, Woodmen of America is a non-profit company, so they reinvest in the community.

I liked that.

Finally I was going to be an earning father again.

But after a few months, I hadn't seen any income, and I was getting a little scared.

I knew there was a bank account Woodmen had had me open when I started, so I checked that.

There was eight thousand dollars in that account! I waited until the next morning and called my supervisor.

"I checked that account and there is $8,000 in there. There must be some mistake."

"I doubt it, but I'll check," he replied. He did, and he was right. That was my money in that account, but I hadn't known it. I was making more money now than I ever had as a cop.

I stayed with Woodmen for a year or so, but one day a man from Mass Mutual called me, offering another position.

Initially, I told them no. I was grateful to Woodmen for how they had helped me after my cop days ended. I had only really considered that one career, and I was lost when it ended. They had given me a new path, and I was very loyal to them.

Though I refused that time, after several calls, the head of the local office got on the phone with me, and we set a date for a meeting.

Mass Mutual and Woodmen are both insurance companies, but the difference is that Mass Mutual would allow me to grow even more and be able to use many fiscal products. I would become a financial advisor, working with clients to maximize their nest eggs, rather than focusing solely on insurance policies.

I liked that. I eventually left the insurance business and went into financial planning, with insurance included, but broadening my own skills and learning to help my clients grow their assets.

I am still there today after several years in the business, and I have taken many additional courses in the field and have earned innumerable trophies for my work with my consumers. I have members of both races as my patrons, and of that I am proud.

I still have my friends – neither black nor white – but friends.

As I have worked on this narrative of my own life and the influences that have shaped me, I have had the luxury of evaluating some of those things.

What matters most in my life?

Family – not just my nuclear family, my siblings and my own progeny – but the extended family in my world. Friends who have literally saved my life in the tough times. Friends who stood by me through financial trials, through legal trials, through social trials. Family often goes beyond the genetic definition and extends to your friends you have chosen to be like family.

Church was the single institution that remained stable during these dreadful times. I would drive out to the cemetery to talk with Dad and Larry – and unfortunately, during my difficult time in 2006 and 2007, they were joined by Bennie. How I missed Bennie, but I knew he, Dad, and Larry were with God.

The members of the church gave me moral support, too.

My church is critical to my salvation through all this. I couldn't have kept my promise to Melissa that I would never kill myself if I hadn't remembered that I was a child of God and suicide would be an action against our savior, Jesus.

But going beyond all those things, I considered the world of law enforcement. It has changed since I started at the tender age of twenty all those years ago.

I think the anonymity of computer and squad car relationships works against the success of keeping a safe community. But, at the same time, technology, DNA, and other scientific advances have enabled investigations to solve cases, both new ones and cold cases from decades ago.

Community policing is, to me, the best strategy around. I keep remembering the black cops whose bullets rusted in their guns. They were the guys who could quell a possible riot by just speaking louder. "James! You. Stop. That. Now! You can't embarrass your momma behaving like that!"

Of course, there are some truly bad guys, and we have to use strong force to get them off the streets, but once you get all those fellows in jail, then you work with the community. And sometimes, the ones whose behavior forces you to throw them on the hood of the car come out of jail, and start a business themselves.

Recently, one of my interns asked me if I would sit in on a discussion with a potential client.

He brought his new client in. "Sit down," I invited the two of them, and they both did.

The guest looked familiar, but I couldn't place him. He looked at me the same way. We both knew that we had met before but were a bit vague on where.

Then he said to the intern, "This guy sent me to jail!"

The intern was more than a little uneasy at this. I know he was thinking, "Uh oh, should I even be considering this guy as a client?"

About that time, I remembered who the guy was and told him so.

"You slammed me up against the car and handcuffed me. You ought to remember."

I apologized for not remembering his face – not for treating him badly.

"I'm fine," he said. "I was wrong. And you did what you had to do. If you hadn't gotten me off the streets, I'd be in prison instead of sitting here trying to figure out my finances for the future!"

He was making over $250,000 per year by owning two trucks and transporting goods from here to there.

I had arrested him more than once…and I still had his respect. What pleased me was that he is a card-carrying successful businessman today.

Community policing is simply a matter of caring about your neighbor. No matter what those folks have done, we are all brothers in this world, and even the most despicable criminal deserves human courtesy. At least that's what I think. And that's how I handled my job. The man who I once arrested and who is now making over $250,000 a year told me that every time we arrested him, he always knew Cliff and I would treat him fairly. That means a lot to me.

I also think a lot about the role of instant decision making in policing. There is no real training for finding yourself in this situation, no matter whether you have been on the force twenty years or twenty minutes.

Sometimes you have to evaluate the situation in a flash and make a life-changing choice. Just ask any of the policemen in Louisville who went in and killed Breanna Taylor; George Floyd in Minneapolis; Tamir Rice in Cleveland, Ohio; Michael Brown, Ferguson, Missouri; or the citizens who jumped in and killed Ahmaud Arbery in South Carolina.

Split-second decisions based on your experience or fear can affect your life for all your days.

And those who are also involved in those decisions will have days, weeks, months, and often years to analyze your actions.

Time you didn't have when you made that decision.

That's something all cops have to recognize as a reality. And all citizens should understand it, too.

Decisions have consequences.

Such decision making brings about another issue I faced: unexpected change. One day I'm living my dream – I'm a deputy chief, I'm earning a good living, and I am respected in my hometown and county.

The next minute, I have been put on suspension – first with pay then, Heaven forbid, without pay!

Talk about an unexpected change in your life.

Cliff Hardy always described things vividly: "It's like somebody reaches in and grabs your guts and your liver and twists them."

What do you do?

I hope no one who reads this has to go through what I did. But at the same time, I discovered the strength that comes from bad things happening.

My removal from the force was not a "tragedy" in my mind. "Tragedy" is what Berta Mae experienced when her son lay dead on his own front steps. Tragedy is losing my friend Rod before he lived to see his grandkids grow up. "Tragedy" is Huzzie and Gurtie dying with their dog in the freezer and the Young kids, Kenneth, Ann, and Charoyal, and their friends burning before they ever saw their adulthood.

"Tragedy" brings other strengths, but what happened to me showed me things I may not have thought about!

I discovered that sometimes, we work hard to make a path that isn't exactly what is best for us. In the long run, the years since 2010 taught me that I was meant to be in another field, that I could use the skills I had built up in reaching across the boundaries of life – whether it be race, religion, or economic status. God knew, I believe, that I would learn from this experience to move forward, not stay in the same spot. I would learn that it's best sometimes to not fight what's happening and go with the flow.

Hindsight is 20/20, right?

That experience taught me that there are lots of good people out there. They saw my situation and rose to the occasion. They helped. And as I said before, they saved my life.

There is a thing called "the Tupelo Spirit", and that is what rose to save me. A cadre of white businessmen and others who saw to it that we didn't starve or lose the house, but survived to see a brighter day.

Integrity – that which Cliff and I worked so hard to instill in the Tupelo Police Department – comes from the individuals and the culture of the community. The definition of integrity that works best for me is, "Integrity is doing the right thing, even when nobody is looking."

Today's Tupelo Police Department has integrity. Chief Quaka has his head in the right place and is working to infuse his department with a culture of integrity. He has his staff working on cold cases and is looking at what has worked to reduce the crime rates in Tupelo in the past. He's a good guy, and I wish him much luck.

I've learned many things during these last seventeen years. From TPD and the FBI, I learned many of the leadership basics I have needed in the time since I started to work outside the department. While each of my jobs has given me its own unique set of skills, I credit my early understanding of what it was to be a good leader to my law enforcement career. Going to CDF was amazing. It was so great to learn what you didn't know you didn't know! Most everyone thinks they know what makes a city or county run, but most folks don't have a clue. It is a complicated and integral process, and we are lucky to have the folks who run CDF in our spaces.

My main lesson at Toyota, besides learning the "Toyota Way" was that sometimes doing the same thing over and over and over again does lead to success.

My second tenure at Tupelo Police Department taught me that sometimes God gives you what you want and you find out it isn't what you needed. I had to go back there to see that it wasn't a place where I could be comfortable. I am no longer a cop, but I needed the closure of this experience to be comfortable with that fact.

Modern Woodmen of America taught me that I didn't need a badge and a gun on the street to protect people from the bad guys. Now I use my skills to protect them from what can happen unexpectedly. Folks need to be prepared for death all through their lives. It can happen any time.

Capital Financial Group of Mass Mutual was like moving from the junior and community college athletic conferences to the NFL. I learned – and continue to learn – real financial planning for people. A lifetime of planning so they can retire at ease, have security as their children grow, and make sure they can become successful citizens themselves. It has changed me and my family: we have traveled through the US and even won a trip to the Bahamas! I'm able to teach my kids to be savers so they will be able to afford to buy their own homes or do whatever they want to. I am a well-rounded financial representative who can give my clients many options based on what they and their family decide is most important to them.

I'm the quarterback of financial services for my clients.

I am in such a much better place. I wish Dad could see what picking up those cans for extra cash has turned into today. And I wish Momma could see what the kid "who wasn't supposed to be" has made of himself.

One last thing I learned – in the state of Mississippi, a misdemeanor can be expunged within two years of sentence completion.

I had no idea. One fair day in 2016, I opened a letter from Jim Waide saying my crimes had been expunged. I hadn't applied for it, nor had I paid the $50.00 fee to have it done.

I was stunned.

For all intents and purposes, the case was totally erased. The court record went away, as far as public access is concerned. Of course, deep in the bowels of some courthouse somewhere is a box labeled "Robert Hall Case", gathering dust behind locked doors. But officially, it never happened.

All I went through in 2006 and 2007 ceased to officially exist. All my efforts to be truthful and honest and make sure my words about not getting a fair case were on record – all those records are gone.

I'm clean. I'm happy about being able to say "no" to the question "Have you ever been found guilty of a misdemeanor or felony?" on an application. I'm okay with that part.

But time moves on, and some thirteen years after the day I walked out of the TPD for the last time, I walked into that place again. I didn't know what kind of a response there would be when I entered. But the new major over investigations, Jerry Davis, had called and asked for my help on a cold case.

Against all my earlier vows, I agreed to come to the new police department building to review the particulars of a certain incident.

Jerry Davis – the detective who had called me – let me know that I could enter by the side door and wouldn't have to go through the public area where the reception desk was. "Might be a bit more comfortable for you," he said.

So, I drove on down, parked my car, and with more than a little bit of apprehension, I let him know I was there. I got out of the car and headed for the side entrance.

"Come on in," he said, as he opened the door for me.

I wish I could describe what it felt like. I was in a different place where technology reigned supreme and where every desk seemed equipped with the latest in everything! Boy, do the cops of today have it better than in 1987! Several screens reflected places around Tupelo, with five or more dispatchers sitting there, watching the city and waiting for calls. No glass-enclosed 8' x 8' cube with a huge old computer and a couple of telephones.

This was not your daddy's police department!

I was almost speechless.

"Want a tour before we get down to business?" Jerry asked. "That case won't get much colder if we take a few minutes to look around. What do you think?"

I couldn't wait.

As we started down the hall, I saw some familiar faces. These were the men who were the young guys, the new hires, about the time I left.

"Hey, Chief!" they called out. "Great to see you again." I almost had tears in my eyes. Others asked, "Robert Hall? You're the guy who put together the SOG thing? We've heard about you. How'd you do it?"

So now I, the "old" guy with a bit of gray hair on my head, was standing in the middle of a small group of eager young faces wearing bright and shining badges, ready to learn about SOG.

As we headed down the hall with the group around me, I took a deep breath and began. "Say, have you guys ever heard of Michael Jordan? He's that NBA guy who played for the Chicago Bulls...."

The SOG Team

Acknowledgements

From Robert

In a book like this, there are many folks without whom it would never have seen the light of day.

Family members come first – those who lived with me through all the struggles of my law enforcement career – and those who have empowered me to have a successful life since. Melissa, my wife, is most important of all. She gave me strength when I had none. My children, Marissa, Terrell, and Brandon; siblings Bennie, Larry, Quinnie, Berta Mae, and Diane; and, of course, my niece Daisy were there through the dark days. Beyond that, I give thanks to Cliff Hardy, my partner at the Tupelo Police Department; my friends at the FBI Academy; and my cousin, Anthony Hill, who is the current deputy chief and of whom I am extremely proud. Tupelo's leading citizens, Jack Reed, Sr., and Jack Reed, Jr., cannot be overlooked. Their support as I was growing in my field, and later through the "troubles" of 2006 – 2010 was immeasurable. David Rumbarger; Jerry Davis; my friends at the Mud Creek Missionary Baptist Church in Saltillo; and the teams from CDF in Tupelo, the Modern Woodmen of America, Toyota, and Mass Mutual's Capital Finances Group, and as well as those who anonymously supported me through the worst of times, quite simply saved my life.

They were all more important to me than I could ever express with mere words.

I think when you are a child, "family" is often defined as being "blood kin." But as you grow older and wiser, you come to realize that family means more than just genetics; it means common interests and values – sharing innermost ideas and fears.

I first met Vaughn Grisham during my cop days when he asked to come ride around with me so he could get a better understanding of the people I interacted with every day. It meant so much to me that someone as accomplished as Vaughn would ask for my insight and invest that kind of time in exploring a different life perspective.

Vaughn was the first person I talked to when I decided I wanted to tell this story, and I'm forever grateful to him for directing me instead to Sandy, who has been the perfect person to put my experiences into writing.

Sandy told me when we began that she was going to have to "crawl inside my head" to tell my story, and she has more than achieved that. From the start, I wanted a partner for this project who came from different backgrounds than me. Sandy not only brought that diversity to our team, but has dedicated enormous care to making sure this work reflected my perspective and experiences.

It is not an empty gesture that I asked Sandy if I could call her "Mom." She came to know me in as much depth as if she had given birth to me. I never feared sharing my deepest thoughts with her. And, she said I could, so I do call her "Mom."

The partnership of a 50+ year old black man and an 80+ year old white woman. We made a great team, didn't we? Who would've thought?

From Sandy

Vaughn said "no" when Robert came to ask if he would write his biography; he was in the midst of another book. "But Sandy can do it," he said. So, Robert turned to me and asked, "Will you do it?"

Never one to turn down a challenge, I replied, "Sure."

The die was cast, and I thank Robert deeply for giving me the opportunity to earn a new skill while living, through his experience, the inequities of our nation's society. It has been my honor.

Kudos to my family who stood by my side as I struggled to learn a new way of writing and bring to fruition a story that has more power than I could possibly have imagined in the beginning. My husband, Vaughn Grisham, held my hand as I fought my way through similes, metaphors, and finding synonyms so I eliminated peevish duplications. My children, Terri, Mike, Cindy, and Tonya, along with grandchildren and great-grands, gave me much support, from advice on other words I could use to bringing tasty food and laughter into the house as I tore up multiple drafts because they "weren't right."

I picked up a "pseudo-sister" in Berta Mae Hall Ruff, who also opened her memories of family to me without restriction. I am grateful.

Neil White cannot go unmentioned, because he taught me how to go from "academic writing" to "literary non-fiction," for which I am grateful – it is an ever so much more interesting story to read this way! And I cherish the freedom from footnotes that characterizes "literary non-fiction." Praises to my two editors, Jeanine Rausch and Sinclair Guenther who bailed me out and taught me to put things in the right order and remember that "less is more." If I ever write another book, I hope you will be part of my team. Carroll Moore, who has the eye for a cover that makes the passerby want to pick up the book and read it. Thanks, bunches, Carroll.

From Both the Authors

We give thanks also to the countless number of people who were resources for the stories of Robert's life, from the Cobbs (those parents of my best friend, Rod, in ninth grade) to Berta Mae (who answered every question Sandy had and fed Robert any time he was there) to Wayne Capp (Robert's daughter's godfather, in faraway Montana). The Reeds – Jack, Sr. and Jack, Jr. — are an integral part of this story, and of our lives. And we would like to thank Doyce Deas and Nettie Davis.

"Thank you" simply is not enough, but what else can we say? There are so many other wonderful people who have unselfishly shared their own experiences and finances and resources that we can only say, "You know who you are."

We send you much gratitude in this endeavor.

While we endeavored to keep the standard of honesty at all times, any errors are ours alone.

Collette Grisham, an invaluable part of our team

Vaughn, Robert, and Sandy, 2021

About the Authors

Sandy Grisham

Sandy was a non-traditional student who got hooked on learning at age 38 and never quit. She is a former secretary, community college teacher, partner to her husband in community development and leadership training, writer, photographer, and world traveler. Chief among her favorite careers are wife, mother, grandmother, and great-grandmother.

Robert Hall

Robert Hall was a police officer for twenty years, during which time he became the deputy chief of the Tupelo Police Department and attended the FBI National Academy. He has also worked with the Community Development Foundation in Tupelo, Toyota Motor Manufacturing Mississippi, Modern Woodmen of America, and Mass Mutual. He and his wife, Melissa, have three children, Robert Terrell, Brandon, and Marissa.

Made in the USA
Columbia, SC
16 April 2025

95285c83-f234-42a0-8928-6467034c7437R01